In Tune *with* Myself

Divine Intervention

TIFFINY N. JONES

Fulton Books, Inc.
Meadville, PA

Published by Fulton Books 2020

ISBN 978-1-64654-035-8 (paperback)
ISBN 978-1-64654-036-5 (digital)

Printed in the United States of America

There are some people whom I would like to acknowledge at this point of my life who, when I was down, encouraged me, prayed for me, smiled at me, uplifted me, and most of all, saw something in me that I didn't. These people are Apostle Thomas Hezekiah, Gregory Washington, Sister Linda Johnson Christina Coultas, Michelle Robinson, Veronica Linder, Arlene Rivera, Madeline Bell-Peak, and Josephine Catanach.

I dedicate my book to the one who kept me all together all my life. He watched over me and still does. He kept me when no one else would or could. He consoled me, he wiped my tears away, he covered me in spite of me, he loved me unconditionally, and he still does. He guided me through the tough times, and he still is, he healed me, he comforted me, he walked with me, his spirit talked with me, he smiled on me, but most all, he never left me. And to you my father in heaven, I give this writing to you—the beginning and the ending! Father, I love you and thank you for everything!

I can't forget the three jewels whom you are going to read about whom are my three grandmothers: Mrs. Jimmie Lee Edwards-Jones, Ms. Alice Betty Lynch, and Ms. Cosetta Bowie-Skinner.

I also want to dedicate this space to Mr. Gentleman (R. W.). Had not God brought you across my path, I may not have finished college, and I may not have never ever known what it really is for a man to truly love a woman with no strings attached, even though I made some very poor choices when it had come to such things as being in a relationship with the wrong guy, or with people in general. I immediately would reflect on how you treated me and remove myself from those toxic and bad relationships. It was those memories of the time we shared together that helped me to get through some of life's most treacherous times, my dear friend. And to God (*Yahweh*), I am very grateful to have met such a soul, and I will never forget you because this is my story and you were in it! I love you! Tiffiny.

In Tune with Myself: Divine Intervention was something that I had come up with because the first book I wrote entitled *Out Of Touch with Reality* and finished back in 2010 was stolen from me. If I remember correctly, I think that there was an event being held at the La Quinta Inn Hotel in which a lady from the church I was attending had set up for those of us who wanted to get our story published, I think met with this guy, and they set this event up to help those like myself to try to get their book published. But little did I know that this guy was a crook. Not only was I the only one he scammed and took money from; there were others, but the sad thing is that he took my book and my money and then he just up and disappeared. Needless to say, that took a lot out of me. That really made me want to just give up and just quit on myself, my life, and my reasoning for writing a book in the first place, in which I will introduce to you why I decided to go on and rewrite it again and the reason as to why I decided to write book in the first place.

It was in the year of 2005, if I remember correctly, when I was living with a relative. I was laying down asleep one night, and I heard in my spirit the word *write*. So when I got up that morning, I was like, "Huh?" *Write*. I was like, "Write what?" So I started thinking what in the world can I possibly write about, and it was then when I had realized that boy, do I have a story to tell.

As I started to write, I remember once when I was back home in Louisiana in my younger years when I was going through a really tough time, a prophet by the name of Thomas Hezekiah—who still resides there—told me some things, in which I can't really remember exactly what we were talking about, but these words he spoke into my spirit: "Tiffiny, tell the story because nobody can tell the story like you can." Those words stayed with me. I did not quite understand what the apostle was saying, but now I see. Nobody can write my story but me because I was there whether I wanted to be or not. I went through it. It's pretty wild, but I was like, "Okay, Father. I got it." And write I did.

I had moved in with a relative because I had just been put out of the women's shelter all because I made the choice to purchase a car that I had needed in order for me to continue to live and make it.

Yes, can you believe that? I was put out of a women's shelter because of something someone else had caused, which made me go out and get another car in the first place. The social worker there had a friend who she apparently either was dating or was involved with whom supposedly was a mechanic. So she gave me his number because my brakes had gone out, and he fixed that. Well, that was okay. That was fine, but the problem had come in when I think my air had gone out, and I asked him to fix. Well, he did. But when I was driving my vehicle, I think, for about a week, it broke down again, and I had no way to get around. I had no other means, no one to help me, and I panicked!

I am a single mother, trying to take care of four babies all under the age of ten. I believed at that time and I needed to keep moving. I had mouths to feed and lives depending on me. I did not have time for this foolishness. So I did the best thing I thought I could do, which was to go and try to get me a reliable car so that I can keep going. I had about two thousand in savings, but it was in the savings account that they had in the shelter, and this dang on social worker was trying to please this damn man by screwing over me and my children and take all the money I had for me and my boys to use once we leave. That was so not right. A social worker was supposed to help people to make those decisions so that they can do better in life, not to fail in life, or not to fulfill their agenda, in which I truly believe was to help this man get money by screwing over us poor women in this shelter who were at our lowest point. Ashamed, if you asked me. But we were women who were abused, stupid, ignorant, and dumb and had no sense. Oh, don't forget, we could not articulate our words well, but I am writing a book with two degrees and working on a third. How about that for being dumb? LOL.

You know, yes, we did make some poor choices, but that does not mean we were stupid or ignorant or less than a human because some of us made choices to want to be loved whether we made the choice being clear minded or not. We do and we did, and in this case, since I'm writing about me and my life, I did that. I didn't mean to deviate off topic much, I just had to go there explaining about as to why I end up leaving the shelter because as I am writing and the more I write, the more some things are coming back to my remembrance.

So the reason why I decided to try again with writing my life story is because I have been through a lot in life, and I feel that what I went through can help someone else make it in life no matter the obstacle, no matter the situation, surely no matter where or what you come from. *You can make it!* So this is why I'm writing this book. Not to get back at anyone and not to feel good about myself by exposing people. That's not how I roll. This just happens to be my life, my story, and what happened to me. And I chose to take the good instead of the bad parts from it just as my daddy David said, "To do and run with it!"

Now the mind-set of those people who hurt me during that time I am unsure, and now that I am forty-four, it really does not matter. What matters to me is that I am here unsinged from the fire that I've been in, and I am okay. It was a hard okay, but I'm okay, and I'm ready to be all that I can be for the right cause and that is helping to give life to those who want it. Simple as that.

So as you go on to read my story and as you go on to read about how certain people did what they did to me, I am telling you the story through my eyes and how it happened. Now whether they meant to harm me or hurt me just because in my younger days I didn't know. Only those people and the good Lord up above knows, but whatever the reasoning meant behind it, it happened, and all I have to say is that I made it because I refused to lie there and let other people continue to misuse and abuse me because they had issues. I chose to take the good out of my life instead of the bad because I wanted to live, love, and be happy and share that light with whoever would receive it.

Like my daddy David said to me once, "The world is full of good and bad. It's up to you to make the choice to either choose the good things or the bad things." He said that you can't dwell on the past and that you have to let that go and keep going, and if there are negative people around, whether they are your friend, coworker, sister, brother, cousin, mother, or no matter who it is, love them from a distance. He told me, "Don't even entertain negativity but to embrace positivity and work for what you want." He also said that if you have lived your life, and you have not accomplished anything, then you can't get mad at anyone but yourself. It's nobody's fault but your own. So after that conversation, I am now writing and completing my first book, *In Tune with Myself: Divine Intervention*.

So sit back, enjoy, but most of all, take from my experiences and learn from it to make you a better you and accomplish the unthinkable. After all, I did. LOL!

Life. That's what I call it! Where do I start? How do I start? Let's see. I am from a small country town in Louisiana called Winnsboro. This is the place to where my humble beginnings began. This is where I learned about a man by the name of Jesus and where I started yearning for him at a very early age. It was as if I knew there was something different about me. But I could not quite understand what. This was where I learned how to mind my manners. This was the place to where I would walk down the street, and if you saw your neighbor sitting outside, you literally had to show them respect by speaking or waving your hands saying, "Hey!" Oh, and please don't let your momma or auntie or somebody who is walking with you, and you don't speak. They would shame you right in front of whoever was around, telling you in a really loud and stern voice saying, "*Speak.*" LOL! It was crucial! But that was once the way of life back then. Well, at least for me it was. You showed respect to your elders, and not only that, but to people. Period. No matter their status, creed, culture, or color. That was a must in my household. And the story continues.

I am the oldest of eight children from my mother's side, six girls and two boys, as well as the oldest child of two girls from my biological father's side.

Life for me growing up in the small town of Winnsboro, Louisiana, was a humbling one, I must say. I don't despise where I come from, nor am I ashamed of it. I say this because most are. I don't despise my humble beginnings. After all, that is what helped shape me into the woman that I am today!

In this story of my life, I will share some tear jerkers as well as some joyous and happy times from my childhood up into my life as it is today. It was no sipping ice tea or drinking freshly made lemonade under the tree kind of life. It was mostly a life filled with pain and heartaches and mishaps after mishaps up until I turned forty years old. Wow! Can you image that? Well, sit back and enjoy the ride because you are in for one. LOL! You may cry, or you may not. However it tends to move you, just let it do what it do! This story is for those who have been through life's most treacherous happenings, waiting and hoping for that day to come, wondering when the sun will shine your way! LOL. For real. For real!

Chapter 1

I can remember those days when the fresh smell of those Louisiana pine trees polluted the air in the yard of my grandmother Mrs. Jimmie Lee Jones. Or was it the crisp clean scent of the pecan trees in my lovely grandmother's yard, Ms. Alice? Or better yet, was it the aroma of moth balls in my grandmother's house, Ms. Cossetta? Well, whatever it was, I was happy, carefree, vibrant, and full of life! I knew no pain. I knew no heartaches of any kind. All that I knew was to be free to roam God's green earth with my long black almost waist-deep ponytails, soaring in the air as I climb up and down those pine trees with no fear, or care of life's issues of any kind.

I was a little black girl with love surrounding me from three of the world's most precious gems: the strong and vibrant red ruby, which means fiery, protection, and prosperity (www.crystalvaults. com); the jazzy green emerald, which means to love and enjoy life to the fullest (meaigs.crystalsandjewelry.com); and the cool, calm, and collected white pearl, meaning a precious thing, or the finest example of something, or purity and innocence (crystal-cure.com), if I say so myself. All three of these women had something that relates to each jewel in their own unique way, in which helped carry me through the storms of this life in combination with the divine creator!

It was the words of my grandmother Ms. Jimmie Lee Jones that told me once that if I had any of her blood, I would keep going, and if I do right, God will help me when I would face the hard trials and the test of these times. And it was the softness of Ms. Alice's tranquil voice along with those big hugs, kisses, saying "I love you," along with soft giggles of Ms. Cossetta Skinner and those tight yet gentle hugs that would carry me on as well as her words of encouragement to never give up and that you are never too old to do anything! She taught herself to play the piano up in age. (I think she was around her fifties or sixties when she learned.)

It was through these three strong women with whom I was able to keep on going no matter the obstacle that life had tend to throw my way and to never lose sight of who I was and who I am! It was through their eyes that I was able to stay in tune with myself! Or just keep it real! LOL! But most of all, it was the pureness of their love that I have never forgotten that helped me try to show the same love to others no matter if you get love back in return.

Oh, how I've tried to hold true to those values because there were many times, in which I have found myself unable to show the same love to some people especially if they have hurt me in any way. Or I have even found myself at times struggling with trying to show love to those who may have hurt other people. What can I say? I am human, you know. But I try. And I still try. I just think that if I had not saw them model what true love was, I probably would not be able to have a heart to want to love and help others, especially when some very unfortunate events happened to me from the age nine up into my forties such as being ejected from a moving vehicle six months pregnant. But before that, having been in a homeless shelter for domestic violence victims and their families on top of losing your home to fraud from a natural disaster. And also, having your husband walk out on you because the struggle had begun to become real, and life was taking a toll on him because he also was in the car accident. I really thought we said our vows for better or for worse, but that was a lie, or maybe I just chose the wrong guy. Maybe I had the right plan but the wrong man! Meaning I had planned to live my life with him and try to fulfill God's calling on my life but that fell through. Oh, did I mention being homeless again and having to go to a homeless program when you have nobody to turn to? Even the church people turned on me as if I was a bad disease with no cure. Oh well! Life!

The only person who encouraged me to hang on day in and day out was my grandmother Jimmie Lee Jones. I was down for about seven or eight years, unable to work, and I could barely take care of my family, but God! He took care of me. It was then at my lowest moment to when I truly learned that having faith and trust in God will indeed get your through. So I do thank God up above for those three beautiful jewels of an example that he allowed me to have for that time that I was allowed to have with them while growing up here on this earth to model strength, faith, trust, hope, and perseverance no matter the obstacle!

Oh, I have to mention that there were some aunties and uncles who showed me love, but the two aunties who pretty much kept me up until my mother and father moved into their own house were my aunt Vanessa and my aunt Johnny.

My aunt Vanessa was my mother's sister, and she was the aunt who would fight anybody who looked at me wrong. She kept me as if she gave birth to me herself. It was that kind of relationship. I do remember my aunt Vanessa keeping me for a while, but then she moved out of state, so it was my aunt Johnny B. Golston who toiled with me and one of my sisters while my momma and daddy were trying to get it together.

Aunt Johnny B was the auntie who loved us so. She, too, had a smile that would light up the world. She was kind, sweet, tenderhearted, and she showed loved to whomever would come by her home no matter their color or status. She was just that type of woman. Aunt Johnny believed in treating children with love and making sure that we were always clean, fed, and happy. I learned from Aunt Johnny how to smile and laugh no matter what happens. I learned through growing up around her to take something bad and turn it into something good. An example would be this.

I can remember walking down that country road from her house about maybe less than half a mile to what we called the dump. It was where everybody would go and throw their trash away in this really big dumpster. And lo and behold, my aunt Johnny went to the dumpster empty-handed and came back with things that she was going to take back to her house and make something beautiful with it. And, boy, she did! It is true. Other people's trash is somebody else's treasure. For the life of me, I could not understand that and that image stayed in my head. LOL! But she kept on going with a smile on her face with me, my sister, and her two daughters, in which we were all close in age back to her house to see what she could do with what she got out of the dump. (Aunt Johnny, if you read this, just know that I am laughing myself off and that I truly do love you and I always will.)

But I learned two things from this. I learned that some things and some people just need a little bit of tender loving care and cleaning up. And the second thing I learned from this was that you can have a beautiful home. LOL! Because she did! LOL!

Now, no, she did not get everything from the dump, but it was just that day I remember we were walking down the country road, and we stopped by the dumpster. So this was when I was learning how to take something bad and make it good. And I am so glad to have had these examples in my life as a little girl.

My aunt Vanessa was also loving, but during that time, she was very young, and she eventual moved away, which was very hard for me. But she had a family of her own, and she was trying to start a life with her children and their dad.

I also had another aunt, my mother's baby sister aunt Terrie, who helped take care of me until she left. She, too, was a part of my life because she played with her nieces and nephews, and she would always tell us right from wrong and whip us when were bad. LOL! But she was the aunt who told me one day that it didn't matter that you may not think your life was like it should have been with your mother and father, but you did have some of us to love you. And this was when I had to look back over my life and realize that she was right and draw from that love from those aunties and uncles who were there during the times they were there until they moved away to live their own lives. So she was right. This conversation with my aunt Terrie helped me see that it does not matter who I thought I should have gotten love from, just as long as you got it, and it helped you to a better you. So I drew from it, and I'm still drawing from it.

Life for me was not grand. I can remember when growing up how I was made to always watch out for my sisters and brothers, go to church, and to always (with very strong emphasis on the word always) make sure that our house was cleaned from the inside out. It was as if being clean and going to church was the only thing that mattered. (But to my surprise, that helped make and shape me into the woman I am today.) So I did what I was told being a child. I had no other choice. I was just doing what I was told.

I can also remember how being an older child was not very easy when coming from a large family of seven children at the time. Later on in my early twenties, another brother had come along. But that was when I had graduated from high school, making it a total of six girls and two boys in whom I loved so very dearly. After all, I spent all my young life, raising just about all of them except the last one. I can remember when I had to hurry up from school during my senior year whether it was raining, sleeting, or snowing just to make it home to watch my baby sister as well as being home to for the others when it was time for them to come in from school. I just did what I was told.

I was a tad bit shy but very adventurous! I was always full of life and happy-go-lucky as a child until I had a run in with my environment, according to Erik Erikson.

So at some point in my life, I got stuck! Was it the part to where I was not able to figure out who I was? Or could it have been that awful rape that happened to me around the age of about nine, which made me lose all trust for humankind especially men, and from that point on, trying to figure out who I was? Or could it have been growing up in domestic violence, that unspeakable word that many have no clue about, whereas others are just too ashamed to even speak about? I had no clue that this was what it was called until I had a few run *ins* myself by being in a couple of relationships.

You see, as you may know, domestic violence is something that most people never talked about, and coming from where I come from, this is something you never talk about. Don't ever because for one reason, for some of us, this was just a way of life for some people.

And you don't tell what goes on in your house especially if you come from a place where it seems like everything and everybody was so well put together as if you were invisible to those issues that seems to really cause us to just be quiet and overlook them as if we are not human such as abuse, in which I have found to be impossible the older I got. My emotions had started to get the best of me, and I had begun to experience the world for myself! I was an emotional *mess*!

May of 1992 came, and I was finally beginning to get closer to my goal! Freedom, that is! I had grown up so sheltered until I had no idea that there was life outside the place where I had grown up. Not complaining about my humble beginnings, it's just that I was so very green to life and trusting. Maybe that is why I ended up in the hot seat of those abusive relationships. Or maybe it was because of those smiles that I saw from three of the world's most precious jewels: the red ruby, the green emerald, and the white pearl. Those were the three lovely grandmothers who showed me to love in spite of, which meant to still be good to others even if they are not good to you.

Or maybe I ended up being in those bad relationships because of the emptiness, longing and craving for something that drove me to almost destroying my life! The craving for affection! I bet you are wondering, *I thought that you got that from the three jewels?* Well, I did, but it was for a short time and then the tenderness, the warm hugs, and kisses quickly and unexpectedly went away. Then the most unbearable and unthinkable thing happened in my life at about the age of eight or nine.

At about the age of eight or nine years old, it happened so suddenly! My innocence was snatched in just a few seconds, in which along with some other things that had happen to me almost destroyed my life! I can remember that horrible thing happening that day when my mother was not home when I had come in from school, and I went across the street to my friend's house with her. (I was told that they were supposed to have been our cousins.) Well, anyway, I went inside their house, and as soon as I walked in close to the kitchen, he grabbed me, took me into one of the bedrooms, he snatched my little pants and underwear off, and he raped me! (This is not easy to talk about because to this day, I still have some type of anxiety about that day. I am not where I was emotionally about that day praise God, and I am still growing and getting better because this rape that happened to me still bothers me at times.) So from that point of my life, I was withdrawn, just pretty much an emotional wreck, and the mistrust for the people had begun!

Growing up in a small country town where everybody knows everybody does indeed has its pros and cons. The pros is that if something happens, especially bad, or if you maybe need a ride or something, or maybe need to borrow a cup of sugar, then you can because the lady next door or across the street will always be willing to give you a cup or two with no hesitation. But then on the other hand, the cons would be if something happens to you really bad like me being raped, or the violence that was going on in my home, then no one would believe you because most would figure that you are lying. And if you come from a halfway decent background like I did, then you would pretty much be called a liar! Oh! Don't be actively involved in the church because then if you told what was going on, then you would be shunned or still looked upon as a liar because such things don't happen to people like me, especially if your mom is a Baptist minister. Oh wait, here is a good one. Did that really happen?

So I grew up and dealt with those obstacles of mental torture and not having a soul whom you can talk to, or who would believe you enough to help you. But then again, I had come from a multiracial background, and I was fighting a losing battle anyway. So I looked different. I was picked on by many people and not liked by some of my peers because I looked different. My hair was long, black, and shiny to almost my waist, and some people would say I was pretty, which would have made it hard for someone to believe that I had something like this going on with me. And then my grandmother was very active in the community, so who would believe me?

You see, my mother's mother was half white, or French, Indian, and black from what I was told from a family member. My grandmother's mother's mother was white from a small town called Bunkie, Louisiana. And my dad's dad's momma was white, black, Indian, and I heard there was some Asian somewhere along the lines, in which I wasn't told until I was forty years old by an aunt and my only living grandmother that I have left. I asked my grandmother why you didn't tell me who I was, and she said well I just figured you didn't need to know.

I mean, I guess it didn't matter, but it sure is nice to know a little something about yourself, and who you are because it helps you identify with who you are as well as accept who you are skin-deep no matter your color or background versus being ashamed of who you are because if you ask me, in which nobody did (LOL), none of us had the power to choose who, when, where, how, and why we ended up in some of the families and environments we come out of. If it was up to me, I would have chosen to come from Queen Sheba or somebody. LOL! I am just joking! For real though! LOL! Okay, I quit! LOL!

So to continue with the story, I had to just keep on going and living as if nothing ever happened, but it was hard when you looked different from most in the community. I mean, my skin color was not all that light like most of my family, but I did have some lightness to my skin, and on top of that, I had really long hair, shiny black hair that reach midway to my back, almost to my waist.

Some of the people liked me, and some did not. Yes, I was teased at school because to some, I did not look black, but I was and I am. This was way of life for some of us who looked different back then especially coming from a place to where there was a lot of negativity going on, and for what? But you either had to roll with the punches by hanging in there and be tough, or get knocked out by harsh words of criticism coming from a small country town in Louisiana. I admit it made my skin tough! Maybe a little too tough because through all the talk of the town and the kids at school picking on you by laughing and calling you all kinds of names, you had to muscle up. So this made my skin even tougher. I was getting ready for the world, and I did not even know it!

I was also taught as a child to not forsake God and his teachings along with trying to be strong-minded and not worry about what was going on around me. For me, learning of a savior who died for the sins of the world and that there is someone who will always love you no matter what is what helped me stay sane through it all and is still keeping me unto this day as I speak! (Thank you, Father! Thank you!)

So guess what I did? When I left home after I graduated from college, I went left the complete opposite when I left home. It took a couple of years though, once I graduated high school and about two years after high school is when I started straying away from my upbringing making not so good choices in my life. It was as if I completely had no understanding of my behavior and why I ended up making some of the choices I did, but that would be about right considering my background, which was religious, strict, and abusive. What a trio huh?

You see, when coming from abuse or a violent environment, this does indeed can, has, and will affect one's well-being and can cause some really serious issues in one's life, if we never seek the right help that is needed in order to live life to the fullest as the Bible says. It will and can be very difficult for someone to reach their full potential! Though not impossible, but sometimes for some, it can be very difficult. So I somehow managed to slip through the crevasses of life, and I did manage to get a nursing degree in spite of all the crazy things that had happened in and around my life. And I was also able to obtain psychology degree as well. (It had to have been divine! LOL! Because God was/is good to me! LOL!)

So I went on through my life broken, abused, misused, mixed up, and confused as well as identiless with not a care in this world if I lived to see the next day or not. I was literally a lost soul just existing and doing what I thought I was big and bad enough to do no matter the cost. I was drifting and floating on the raft in what I call my ocean of hurt and pain while all at the same time being surrounded by vicious and ferocious flesh-eating sharks, waiting to eat me alive! (But God!) Oh! How I wrestled with myself back then, and oh, how I wrestle with myself now.

But the difference between now and then is that I am mentally free! The struggles that I have today are not as nearly bad as those struggles of mental bondage as the struggles to keep going when sometimes you want to give up. I mean, I am in a better place mentally, and I thank God in heaven for helping me and not ever leaving me when I just knew I was going to completely lose my mind. That comes later in the story. So it would be those struggles of recovering from unfortunate events of life that I am talking about. But as I mentioned, that comes later.

I almost let what happened to me in my past life consume me! I made choices based on how I was feeling. I made choices based on being hurt, abused, and misused. I made choices based on what I thought of myself to be, which was not too much of anything, but to be somebody's rug mat to walk on and just lay there and take it until I get angry enough to tell them off or to disassociate myself with them by holding grudges against them and not budging no matter how they would try to come back and talk to me. Instead of me having a heart to forgive, I chose to hold what they did to me hostage and not knowing that I was killing myself softly inside without a care in this world. I did what I thought was pleasing to myself out of pain and hurt.

You see, when you grow up in a place or an environment where it seems as if the word nothing is your dearest friend, then life would really look bleak. Living life would be like one just drifting from sea to sea in hopes of somebody coming along to save you, and in my case, no one did. I had to rely on my own strength within as well as my faith in my father in heaven. In which is what helped me get through those tough times and even now to this day.

As a child, life for me was very bitter all the way up to my teens. I had no enjoyment. I had no life. I went to school, church, and back home, then from there, cleaning and babysitting as if that was all for me. I was shown that my life was nothing, and I better not try to believe any different because as far as Tiffiny was concerned, nothing is all she better think about. Only certain people in life could be happy and live life to the fullest. Not Tiffiny. Not her. It was just the way it was for me at one point.

It was as if all of a sudden, every happy moment that I once knew was snatched from me with no warnings at all. But no matter how I was treated, I still managed to smile and show loving-kindness to mankind. It was as if I was wired to do so. In spite of the trauma that I endured as a child from being raped and abused in just about every way possible, for some strange reason, I managed to come through the fires of hell on earth unsinged. It was as if I came out fighting to not let what happened to me define me. (I thank God too!)

I have to admit, it was not easy because by the time I was a sophomore in high school, I had no more reason to live. I was alone in my parents' home, sitting in the nice and clean living room on the floor next to a glass table with a big butcher's knife in my right hand, and I put it across my left wrist, pushing it down, trying to cut myself. But as I was pushing down, for some odd reason, I stopped! It was as if something inside me was saying, "Don't do it!" (It had to have been divine.) So I put the knife down, and I cried, in which crying was so very rare for me because I didn't cry.

You see, when you grow in an environment where abuse is present, sometimes some of us will tend to become numb to the world outside us. You tend to become cold and withdrawn and oh, did I mention, no smiling or no reactions to a smile at times in certain instances such as someone smiling at you just because. But your response is dry and callous and everything that else that associates itself with that word numb. I was like that for some time in my life, but for me, those feelings of despair and numbness got lost somewhere. Maybe it was those smiles of those beautiful jewels that I mentioned previously. Maybe if I had never experienced what a drop or an ounce of love was, I think that I would have gone past the point of no return in my psych! LOL! (Praise God!)

I feel like I would have been heartless, cold, and continuing to live my life with those out-of-control self-sabotaging behaviors that would have literally destroyed my life! Needless to say, for about seven or eight years of my life, I went on in my life broken and confused with not a care in this world if I lived or died because of me feeling myself! (Meaning I was drowning in my own sea of despair because it was all about me and my feelings and making sure that I pacified those feelings as well as wearing them on my shoulders, until one day, I had a real encounter with the divine creator!)

I was twenty-three years of age, and I was living my life as though there was no tomorrow. Although I was brought up to be

21

a very decent young lady with morals and values, I went the total opposite of how I was raised. I went from going to church service on Sunday, Monday, Wednesday, and sometimes almost every day of the week to a club-hopping, beer drinking, and getting high individually, and most of all, I loved it! If someone with any of God's Word in them would approach me and try to tell me any different, or tell me that I need to go to church, then I would say to them with a smile, "Don't tell me what the Bible says. I already know what it says. If you want to tell me something, say something nice to me, or I would also say be kind to me." (Not knowing that I had been through some very harsh things in my life, growing up in the environment that I had come from!)

You see, when and a person grows up the way I did, life can kind of be really confusing. For one, it's because of me going to a very Southern Devout Baptist Church and learning that the God we serve is loving and kind, but when you go home, life was pure madness! And not only that; there were some of those same people going to the same church I went to, laughing and making fun of me and my family, saying such things as I didn't think preachers have problems, which really made me hot inside. But because of how I was brought up, I had to stay in my place and not sass a grown up. (I used to hear that growing up. Don't sass me meaning don't be disrespectful, or talk back to an adult when you are a child.)

So in going to church almost every day of the week to going to a place to where there was fighting and arguing, pulling shotguns, seeing one parent stab the other parent, and having women come walk right in front of your house while you are out playing, wanting to fight your mother over her husband while your mother was out-side in the laundry room, washing her family's clothes, minding her own business was a bit much to endure as a child. And I am quite sure as a wife as well, but this was my life, and my story as to what I saw from a little girl's eyes. Whatever and however this came to be is unknown to me. All I know is this is what happened, and this is how life was coming from a small country town in Louisiana in Tiffiny's environment. No wonder I went from the church to the club. I was becoming what I come from in a negative way at first, until my life took a turn for the better one day. I will explain later on in the story.

As I was saying previously, I was a mess! An emotional mess! I did not know who I was, or where I was going, just drifting from place to place running from what? I had no clue. Maybe it was the life that I had once knew as a child, or maybe I was running from myself, or maybe I was running from the truth, and I did not want deal with the truth. And maybe that was because I had no idea on how to deal with the truth, and I kept running until I ran into the wrong hands, which could have literally destroyed my young life! (Here we go again! But God! He kept me once again.) I was so foolish and very naive! I was living my life on the edge without hopes of a future, just living in the moment.

College came. Really? Tiffiny, going to college? Well, do you know maybe there is hope for Tiffiny after all? So yeah, I ended up going to college for about two years until I just got tired of all the pressure from my mother. I mean, my mother depended on me for almost everything. Maybe it was because she had had me at such a young age, and she never had no one else she could cling on to with the strength that I had besides her mother. Or maybe it was because she never wanted me to get close to no one because maybe in her mind, someone may take her daughter from her who was her backbone. What I mean by this is ever since I was old enough to get a job, I worked, and every money I earned, it went to her, in which I did not mind. But here is where the problem had come in at. You see, when I left home to go to college, I applied for a job in my freshman year so that I can work to help myself. But every weekend, my mother was there, making sure that I come home so that I could help her pay her bills when I was trying to help myself make it through college. I did not mind helping her. I was trying to make it in the world for myself, and it was too much pressure for me because just about all my entire life, I devoted it to her by not having a life growing up.

You may wonder, *Was she sick, or had a health condition?* Well, the answer is no. She just had me at a young age, and I was the one who she left all seven of her kids with day in and day out, trying to figure out where my dad was and why he never came home. So it was as if she had a hold on me, in which I could not shake until I got up the nerve to leave the state in hopes of a better life. But even that did not work because I ended up going back home because of her always needing help on top of her not wanting to see me happy because every time I would try to date someone, or try to have a relationship, she would always find some way to try to sabotage it.

It was not until years later until I realized that when I met this really nice young man who cared about me and wanted to help me make something out of life, but it was her and another family member that let jealousy rise up in them, and they came in between the one true and only love that I had ever encountered whom was next to God. Mr. Gentleman and I were a lot alike, and for the life of me I could not understand how something all so so right could turn out all so so wrong. But what I did not know was that Mr. Gentleman had a dark secret of his own. He hid it well underneath his charismatic smile and his outgoing personality until no one would have ever thought that he could have endured such hardships while growing up.

I mean, he was, again, as I mentioned previously, this tall, fine brown-eyed brown-skinned brother who played college ball, had a college degree, his own crib, and he was single!!!!!! And most of all, he treated women with the utmost respect as if he was never affected by the terrible and horrible things that happened to him while growing up in his young life. He was beautiful inside and out, but most of all, he liked me. But most of all, he treated me with respect, in which no other man or no other relationship I was in made me feel the way I did and still do to this day about Mr. Gentleman. Who would have known that he, too, was molested by a family member or members? (One was a woman.) No wonder he and I clicked. We were both broken, and it was as if we unknowingly understood each other unconditionally and automatically. Okay, let me slow down. I'm getting ahead of myself.

So I was in my second year of college, and I did not apply for a job that year on campus because she would end up threatening me or trying to fight me because I would not give her my whole paycheck. So I did not apply. Instead, I ended up calling a relative of mine, asking her if I could come live them to try to go to school where they lived. And lo and behold, what I did not know was that I was going to run into that ugly thing called abuse again, in which I never thought that this particular relative would never do because they were so well looked upon from being a high achiever all at the same time having some deep-rooted issues on the inside that really came out when they saw something good was happening to me. It was as if this certain relative really did not want me to succeed. It was as if they wanted to see me fail because of the domineering, controlling, and abusive behavior that they exhibited.

But needless to say, because of their accomplishments in life, no one would believe me. No way. Because for one, I was a small time country girl whom did not do to well in school. I was soft-spoken. Self-esteem was on a negative scale of negative zero. Not zero but negative zero if there is such a scale. On top of that, being rejected by your parents was rough and in the back of my mind at one time I had wished what was told to me, which was I wish you were never born while hearing some of the things that were said to me as a child. I would think the same thing. I wish I was not born either. It was not like they all were doing me a favor because as far as I can remember, when I was old enough to work, I worked, which was in the eighth grade. And if my grandmother did not help me along with a couple of relatives, giving me their children's hand-me-down clothes, I probably would have committed suicide because it was so very painful to come up and live through what I did. Abuse, rape, being laughed at, and talked about at school, and then having to go home and take care of babies I did not have on top of being called dumb, stupid, and nothing. That was mental torture. But there was and is a God that had and still have his hands on me.

And so when I went to live with this particular relative, I really looked up to them, and I had a lot of respect for them. But that respect I had left me when they showed their true colors when something good was finally happening for me. I mean, I forgive that relative, but throughout the years, I had lost respect for that person, but because of the act that was done to me out of pure jealousy when I went to live with them and them not wanting to see me do well in life all because they thought that I was not good enough for something good happening for me because they said it out of their own mouth. (*Family!*) And you know what? It has been years on top of years, and I am not mad. I wish them well. You see, when you try to sabotage another person's life and then laugh about it, that's cold. Heartless, if you ask me, in which nobody did. I'm just saying. It was just callous. But that's life. And again, I am not mad anymore, and I still do wish them well. All you have to do is try to pick up the pieces and move on as best you can with the help of God. Okay, enough of that.

So I stayed with this particular relative. I was already feeling down on life, low self-esteem, and not a friend in the world with whom I could confide in. All I had was my faith and hope in God, feeling down on myself, not knowing which way was up or down. I was pretty much a lost cause, or so people said. I say this because my mother had come to me one day and said something to me that really hurt me. She said, "You know what people are saying in this town?" I just looked at her. She said, "They said that you ain't gon' graduate high school, and you gon' end up having a lot of babies." Well, coming from what I come from, they were right, but that did not happen. I did graduate high school with no babies. Ha! How about them apples? LOL! Anyway, I was really down inside, and I thought that by changing the scenery would help, but it didn't. It only made things worse. But I end up encountering a being at that point of my life with positive vibes who had left a great impact on my life for the rest of my life!

So I made it safe and sound to my relative's place. It was nice, quiet, and subtle, something that I needed form years of abuse and negativity. It was a breath of fresh air, in which felt good to my soul. I made it, and they were very happy to see me. They even introduced me to their friends and even let me use the car to go back and forth to work. And I was trying to get back in college because that was something I always wanted to do—to go to college and finish. But because of me having a very controlling and forceful parent trying to run my life. What did I know about life? I was green, naive, and country with no sense of the world or any sense of how to go out in the world and function. All I knew how to do was to keep house and mind my manners with my head held down low with no hopes of nothing good ever happening to me. But God! LOL!

It was a warm and sunny day when my relative and I went to hang out with their friends. It was strange for one because I was never really just used to going out, hanging with people, or socializing much because I was made to stay inside while growing up and taking care of my siblings, so I felt awkward needless to say that there was this guy there who really got on my nerves! He literally made me upset. First of all, I thought that he was rude because we got into that same day I saw him. I can't exactly remember how the conversation went, but I do remember him, and I was going at it right there in front of everybody in the mall. And I did not care because he had gotten on my nerves.

So that day went on, and lo and behold, that same guy who was at the mall ended up taking me out, showing me the town per my relatives request. Well, so they said. I was not for sure if he asked to show me around, or if my relative asked him to take me out like a kid sister thing. You know what I mean? It was supposed to have been a big-brother-little-sister deal, but that is not at all what happened. Keep reading and follow me. You will see what I mean.

So I hung out with Mr. Rude, and, boy, did we hang out! LOL! Every week we're hanging. He would call and say, "Ask your family if I could take you out." And he would ask me if I wanted to go, and to my surprise, I said yes! I say this because at first, I thought that he was rude, and I wanted no dealings with him even if was just riding up the street and back. I just did not like him, but to my surprise, Mr. Rude turned out to be okay. I am laughing hard right now because to picture how we met, you would laugh too. LOL!

So the days and the weeks went by, and we were hanging tough. It was getting to where we were inseparable. I mean, we would shoot pool, we would go to events, and we would hang out there, and everybody was watching and wondering what was it about that broke no-having-nothing-country-and-naive girl and Mr. All-having-money-crib-car-college-degree-played-college-football were doing. Maybe it was the bounce if my cold shiny black hair, bowlegs, red skin, pretty smile, brown eyes, nice little track-shaped legs, small petite frame of a body, along with that carefree spirit that drove him, or maybe it was true love! Whatever it was, it was real, something that I had never felt in life, and it felt good. And we were not having sex! *Ah!* LOL!

Seriously, we were just hanging out. It was cool. It was nice, happy, refreshing, respectful, and most of all, loving. I had never felt that way especially coming from the toxic environment I had come from. It was so unreal to me! Something good happening to me? Really? Well, as you know, all things come to an end, good or bad. Well, at least for me.

I can remember calling my mom and telling her that I had met someone, and I thought she would happy for me, but that was a bummer. She told me that I needed to come home, and for the life of me, I could not understand that. What? Tiffiny could not be happy and have somebody like her for real without trying to use her? I can remember she went so far as to calling this lady who was a prophet, asking her about the guy with me on the phone, and to my surprise, the lady said, "Yeah, he is the one for her." She told me to come home, and I said, "What?"

I can also remember that one day I was working at this hardware store, and there was this strange-looking man who had walked by me, wearing a crystal around his neck. And he stopped and asked me if he could tell me something. And I said, "Yeah, you can." I had never seen him before, nor did I ever encounter such soul as him. I can remember him telling me, "There is this thing about you and your mother and your boyfriends, and she is always telling you that something is wrong." He said something else, but it was so long ago, I can't remember. But what I do remember is that he was trying to tell me that she was still trying to sabotage my happiness, and me being country and green, I had no clue to what he was saying until years later when I ended up losing him to someone else. But that's not how I ended up losing him at first.

Seven years later, I had gotten back in touch with him through an old work number I had ran across, and I called his friend to ask where he was. And the friend told him about me, and we ended up getting back in touch with him and being his girl again. But I ended up losing him to something that I thought that would never happen. I'll tell you later.

The first time I ended up losing the love of my life was when my relative who started all this in the first place started to get really mad, jealous, and upset because we were hanging a little bit tight. This particular relative had started really making it hard for me to stay there. She kept pressuring me to get my own place and to go talk to other guys, in which this guy was very good to me. I had gotten a job, I had gone to try to get back in college, but by me being out of state, I had to pay this really big out-of-state fee. And then on top of that, I had no clue on how to fill out financial aid papers, in which that relative did, but I don't remember her trying to help me. But instead, this relative started insulting me and talking down to me and saying such things as "You are just a mother ready to happen," and I was not even having sex!

In my mind, I would like to know how that was going to happen because I did not just sleep with guys. But anyway, that relative would then shift to try to fix him up with other women. I can remember that he once told me, "Your relative said, 'Tiffiny don't have nothing. Why get with her?'" He also said that she is a big whore, in which I was not doing nothing but working and hanging with my friend, the one she introduced me to. So needless to say, I ended up having to leave.

My relative was really giving me a hard time and really fussing at me, telling me I had to leave. For some reason, that relative was really upset with me once me and Mr. Gentleman was getting too close to each other. There was a side of that relative I did not know existed. She had become really verbally and emotionally abusive, like I really needed that at this point of my life being that this is what I had come from. And what I did not know was that Mr. Gentleman, yes, turned out to be the perfect gentleman for me was also hurt, in which I did not know.

I say this because twenty years later, I kind of ran into him again. (*Whoa.* LOL. Three times a charm, huh?) And he told me that the week he went out of town for his job, he had made up in his mind that we were going to be together and that he had planned to take me out of state with him and help me get back in school and we were going to live! He also told me that when he had come back to town, he went by my relative's house, looking for me. And he said, "When that relative had come to the door, they laughed and said, 'She went back home.'" And Mr. Gentleman said, "What you mean she went home?" In which I didn't. I had just moved a few hours away from him with another family member. He told me that tore him inside and that he went to was torn up inside and that the position that he was supposed to take he didn't and that it was another coworker who ended up with the job.

Two people's lives affected all by what someone else thought should or should be or maybe because someone wanted Mr. Gentleman for their own self but was using me for a cover up, and when their plan backfired on them, they got really furious inside and decided, "Hey, it's time for you to go."

You see, it was meant for a joke because when this relative set this little hang-out thing up, they laughed about it to my face. Wow! We humans are something else aren't we? LOL. I am so glad that God is not like that because if so, we would not have a chance for hope, peace, love, and most of all, forgiveness! Oh! Did I mention that yes, I forgive that relative, and this is my story, this is what happened, and this was my life once upon a time.

And there I was, thinking that he didn't care, or he really didn't think much of me, but he really did. Oh, well. *Life!* So I was forced to leave. I mean, I could not get an apartment because I was making minimum wages, and I had no clue as to how to get my own place and my relative, for the life of me, had stopped wanting to help me make it. It was as if their thoughts were, *Who do you think you are to bring your broke-nothing-having self up here, trying to have somebody with something?* It was as if I could only go so far and, in this case, just to hang out like brother and sister, in which I did not know that I had to have an approval on who I fell in love with. But that's how it was with me and certain ones in my family. Not all but some. And that is what happened.

You know, come to think of it, I remember coming in one day from work, and my relative and Mr. Gentleman were sitting down, having dinner together. I could not believe it. If I remember correctly, I think that my relative asked Mr. Gentleman if he could come over and have dinner together. And he, being the carefree, down-to-earth guy he was who got along with almost anybody, agreed. I mean, he was looking at it like a friend thing, but that girl's intuition was not having it! But hey, no assumptions! But I never said anything because for one, I was in their home, and I was raised to not disrespect people in their own home especially if I was a guest.

So I went on as if nothing happened. I was crushed and so I walked outside, and he called me and asked if I could come by and we could hang out. And I did because by that time, he was my friend. A true friend. I guess that I could not get mad because he was tall, standing six foot three with beautiful light-brown eyes, built like a football player, small waist, and nice hips and thighs. *Oh Lord!* He was divine and then when he would smile, it would just light up my world. And he was a gentleman to me. He was really nice to me with no hidden agenda to harm me. It was pure and innocent. Oh well, that was cut short.

And had I known that he really liked me and really wanted me to be his love, I would have never left him. I would have camped out by his doorstep until he had come home because a love like this is so hard to come by. This was real love. I mean true love. A love that those around us could not comprehend. It was something so real that we clicked, and we understood each other without having to go to bed with each other, or even really having a conversation about what we were doing, where we were going, or almost anything. It was as if we just understood each other automatically. We would listen to Teddy Pendergrass, Betty Wright, and Bobby Womack while he would stand in the doorway, singing "I love you" as loud as he could while I sat down on the floor, looking and laughing at him, trying to sing to me, not knowing that he really did love me.

Now that I look back at it, he did love me, and I could not even see it because of me not believing that nobody could ever love me besides the ones I mentioned in the beginning of my story. Life! He would take up for me if somebody did me wrong. He was always there for me when I needed him. He encouraged me to love myself and to always take care of myself and to always get something for myself, in which I did. Thanks to him and the good Lord. It would have been nice to have had him in my life. But because of what was going on around me, I had no control, and I had no clue on what to do. So I left.

I ended up moving in with another relative in another city because I had to go. I could no longer stay with that relative because something good was happening for me, and they could not stand it. So you see, why did I say what I said earlier? Yes, I forgive them, but I have no respect for them because if a person's heart is right inside, then it does not matter who gets what. But for some, they only think that there is a limit on who gets what, and in that case, they made it perfectly clear that this was something that was not going to happen. And thanks to this relative and my mother, I ended up losing the one thing that made me truly happy at that point of my life and that was Mr. Gentleman.

So I ended up leaving the area where Mr. Gentleman was, and I moved to Las Vegas with my aunt and uncle out there who were really nice to me. But of course, Vegas was too fast for me by me being a small-time country girl. So needless to say, I stayed for a while, worked, and I enrolled in a collage out there.

Everything was going good. As a matter of fact, things were going so good until I had met again another guy. No, I did not go out to Vegas, looking for love, or looking for someone. It just happened. After all then, during that time, I was told I was very attractive, and I did have guys trying to get with me. But I was not interested until this tall, dark, and smooth-talking young man. He saw me, and he was interested in me. He had come to my uncle's house and asked me if he could take me out, and there it went. I did. I mean, he was not forceful with me. He was really nice to me. He was so nice and full of life and always smiling, and I really liked him until I ended up moving with him. (Oh my god. I committed sin!) A preacher's daughter out there in Las Vegas, doing God knows what.

So I ended up moving in with him, and, boy, did he know how to treat a girl. He was good to me, but again, that relationship was cut short. I think I dated him for about a year and then I left. I ended up getting pregnant, and when my mother heard, she said, "It's best you come home." Well, I said to myself, *No, I'm not gon' mess this relationship up*. But guess what? I left anyway.

She told me, "You need to come from out there, and if you don't, something bad was going to happen to you every day until you come home." I was like, "Yeah, right." Well, as soon as I got off the phone with her, I almost got into a fight with these two girls over some guy I used to talk to, and I never saw that guy since who knows. It was just crazy! So I left. I think I left the next day. I did not tell him or anybody.

I was hurt and crushed, and I felt like there was no hope for me. I was pregnant, and I could not take care of a child. And my mother was wishing bad on me and for no reason. So I went home to nothing. I went back to a place that someone like me could not thrive in because of what I was carrying and that was something bigger than myself.

So I tried to go to school and work, but my mother made it very difficult for me to stay at home. So I ended up coming home and being homeless. I mean, I stayed for a while, but she was giving me hell and charging me rent. Whatever happened to I made a mistake, and I will help you? *No.* Not me. I was the worst thing that ever happened, and there was no such thing as a mistake. Oh well, I did the best I could to try to please her until I got tired, and I eventually left again.

I got tired of being treated like God doesn't love me and that he only loves certain people. So I said, "F—it. I'm out." So I ended up going back to Texas and ended up meeting Mr. Gentleman again. And this time, that particular relative was not around. And we enjoyed each other's company, and we pretty much were okay. Things were going good until one day, I think I got a call from my mother, or either I called her, and she said, "You are back on the nursing list, and you should come home." I was like, "Man, this was a chance for me to get back in school so I can do really good because I always wanting to finish college, but I just had so much going on with me and in my life until I didn't know if I was coming or going." So I told Mr. Gentleman, and we both agreed.

With tears in his eyes, he said, "There she goes again, leaving me." This time, my mother finally met him, and when she did I ended up not seeing him again. The relationship was cut short. I say this because I can remember one day, Mr. Gentleman had come to visit me from out of town because I had eventually moved back home to finish nursing school. So he would drive ten hours to see me, pick me up, and take me back to visit when I was on a break, and it was then when I saw that this man really loved Tiffiny. But of course, there was my mother. I never saw this coming. I had no clue that she would, or could ever do this to me. After all, I was the daughter who helped her, stood by her, and really loved her whether she was right or wrong, and for this to happen was beyond me. After he left me that time, I never saw him again.

I told her he was talking about really being with me as a wife, and when I told my mother to get her blessing, she said, "Tell him to come eat." I was like okay. I mean, the woman could cook, but me being so damn naive, I had no clue that I was going to lose him again and a chance at something that could have been good and pure. That was that. Maybe he was fixed, maybe it was the food. I am not sure, but whatever happened, the love of my life left me once again. I did hear from him a couple times after that, he just all of a sudden stopped calling me. (Tears in my eyes now, and my heart ached because I could have been with someone who could have helped me become the best me because I was really trying to find myself, and all it seemed like I was getting was hating people around me, trying to sabotage everything I do, and for what? So I lost him.) Life! I couldn't believe it! Two family members in whom I looked up to at one point in my life deliberately and deceitfully destroyed something that was so beautiful out of bitterness and jealousy. (And if you ask me, it was pure evilness. Oh well. Life!)

So I went on to finish nursing school in spite of what I was told especially by these two family members. You know, when I went to live with the relative who introduced me to Mr. Gentleman, he told me that she did not think I was good enough because for I was young, broke, and I had come from the backwoods country. He said that he was asked, "Why would you want someone who comes from a gutter?" And then he said, "People would tell me, 'look how she dresses. You want to be with somebody like that?'"

Now for the life of me, I did not understand why this particular relative would say something like this because for one, she, out of all people, was from the exact same place I had come from. Well, we lived in a brick house, a brand-new one at that. You know, during that time, if you lived in brick house, you were considered to have a little something, but we did not. God just blessed us with a nice home.

And then on top of that, I remember my momma taking food out of our house to help give her bags of food so that she could be encouraged to finish college, in which she did, and in which I am so happy for her. While she was getting bags of grocery, me and my six sisters and brothers would sometimes fall short of meals and have to eat cornbread and milk, just so she could have something in school because at the time, her mom was a single mom, and my mother took the initiative to help out. And to this day, she turns up her nose at my mother, according to my mother. Now, ain't that some stuff? (Not what I really wanted to say, but you know, I have to be respectful and mind my manners as I was taught.) I guess that that's how it is, huh?

Oh well. Needless to say, I went on in life, trying to do the best that I could from where I had come from, which is the gutter, according to the relative. LOL! You know, come to think of it, this same relative talked so bad about me until one day when I was at the apartment, she had a friend or an associate that she was associating with told her to ask me if I could watch her baby while she and her husband goes out. I said yeah because note, I grew up being the oldest of eight children, and babysitting was something I was accustomed to. And this relative had the nerve to say, "You are a mother waiting to happen."

Now again, for the life of me, I could not understand why this relative with whom I looked up to and admired would turn and say such things to me. I was younger than her, and I had two years of college under my belt and was trying to start new when I went to live with her so that I could finish college, but it was as if she fought me on every hand. I should have known when she didn't help me fill out paperwork for financial aid, in which I, at the time, had no clue as to how to fill out the paperwork. It did not dawn on me until later in life why she did what she did. Everything was fine until she introduced me to Mr. Gentleman as a joke, not knowing that we would both end up falling head over heels for each other. And then this is where the problem had come in.

Chapter 2

Life after Mr. Gentleman

Well, needless to say that, that relative won. Everything that she was set out to do regarding trying to sabotage a good thing from not wanting to see me make it in life while I was staying with that particular relative worked in their favor. After all, I was living with the relative, and I had no clue as to how to make it on my own because I had come from a very strict and sheltered background. I did not even know how to pay a water bill, let alone try to get a place of my own.

Yeah, I did work at an auto part store, but it was not enough to keep gas in a car if I had one. So I did the best that I knew how while staying there and trying to figure me out, life, and Mr. Gentleman. You know, I had some really serious emotional issues that needed to be dealt with, and for the life of me, I could not understand why that relative could not understand it. I mean, they were really smart— well, academically smart—but I guess during that time, they had no clue on how to help a wounded girl who was abused and misused. I guess that I needed a shrink then. LOL!

Oh well, I did the best I could, but that was not good enough because my relative started complaining about me to someone on the phone. And then she had begun to become verbally abusive to me as if I had not gone through enough abuse while growing up. But what did she care? Life! So I ended up leaving and moving with another relative in another part of the state. This relative kind of knew something was going on, but she did not say a word, and neither did I. You know, that's what some family members do. Well, at least some of mine did. I guess it was to keep the peace, and that we did, but on the inside, I was hurting. I was torn up. I had been through so much during my life, and finally, I had met someone whom I thought could help bring out the best in me and to help me achieve the unimaginable in my life, but it was taken away from me.

You know, some years later, I had gotten back in contact with Mr. Gentleman, and he said that he did not know what had happened because he haven't heard from me. He said that he went over to my relative's apartment to see where I was, and he said that my relative told him I was gone. And he said, "She's gone? Where did she go?" Mr. Gentleman said that my relative said, "She went back home." He said, "She went back home?" He said that he said it in a very upset voice, and he also said that my relative had a smirk on their face when they said it.

Now, I am writing this being as transparent as I can. I am writing this as it happened. Now whatever the reasoning behind what happened, only that relative can answer that, but human behavior sometimes shows how a person really and truly feels deep inside about someone. That's just like what the Bible says, "Not everyone who says to me, 'Lord, Lord,' will enter the Kingdom of Heaven, but only the one who does the will of my father who is in heaven." Matthew 7:21. The Bible also mentions how "God looks at the heart and not what we may tend to see about people." 1 Samuel 16:7. Meaning just because this relative introduced me to this person, it did not mean that they really wanted me with him, nor did they want me happy because their behavior showed it.

So Mr. Gentleman told me that he was hurt and that he had no closure and that we were getting alone good and that I was getting ready to get in a place to help you. It was at that moment then that I realized he was too in love with me just as I was in love with him. Life. I told him that if I could turn the hands of time back, I would.

I told him that if I had known that I was going to go through life without him in it, I would have stayed and camped at his doorstep, meaning I never would have left because for once in my life, I had someone besides those three jewels and with the exception of aunts and uncles who loved me dearly. So I went on with life, trying to make sense of what had happened, and I went on lost and confused, not knowing what to do. So I kept moving from place to place, trying to find me and my purpose for living with a hole in heart.

I moved to and forth, from city to city, and state to state until I finally gave up, and I went home. I ended up being pregnant at around the age of twenty-three with my first son. I really was confused. I was from place to place, and man, when my mom found out, that was the worst thing that I could have done. Yeah, I was home then and living with her. I had received no support, none whatsoever from her. Let her tell it. If it were up to her, she told me that I would not be having that. That's what she said to me. I just bowed my head, and I cried. I mean, maybe she had high hopes for me, or maybe she didn't because as far as I could remember, when I told her how happy I was and that I met someone really nice when I was living with that particular relative at the time, she told me that I needed to move back home. I immediately said, "What?" I really thought that she was happy for me, but come to find out, she, too, was trying to sabotage my happiness, in which happened most of my life with her, but I did not know that until now.

It took me until now to see that it was my own mother, whom I ate with, who did not want to see me happy in life. I say this because for a long time, I could never have anything, I could never be stable in nothing, nor did I have any peace as long as she was in my life. I mean, maybe it was her way of showing love, but whatever it was, it was literally destroying me inside and out. I tried for years and on top of years to do everything she wanted and how she wanted until I had come to grips myself with God's help. It took me waking up and seeing the truth for what it was and that was the woman who birthed me had a hard time accepting me. Crazy, huh? I know it, but there are many others out there who went through worse.

Well, I guess she tried. I mean, I have forgiven her, and I still love her, but as far as me and her having a mother-daughter relationship, we really don't. And I truly believe and feel in my heart that it will never happen. You know, when a child is born, it's up to the mother and father to give the child those necessary tools to succeed in life, or to be all that they can be effectively and productively with God's help. And in some cases, there are those who honestly have no clue on what to give their child or children in order for them to reach their full potential at life because they may have never been given what they needed themselves so that they could show their child/children something different and/or better. And that's some of the reason why we have so much chaos in our world today. Note, I am not saying this is the reason why so much craziness is happening in our world today. I mean, just some of the reasons why, and until we all come together and try to make this world we live in better, then change, which sometimes may seem strange, will never come.

I'm a parent now, and I do have somewhat of an insight on what it is to try your best to raise up a child so that they can reach their full potential in life and that you have to be emotionally and mentally stable to try to raise a child especially in today's world. But what's a man or woman to when they can only do what they can from what they are accustomed to especially if they come from the side of life to where you have to go for what you know emotionally as well as mentally, which could mean some very dysfunctional and screwed up stuff. But God! LOL! But God!

My reason for saying this is because I had to fight, persevere, and push myself mentally as well as hold on to my faith in God, in whom I was taught about as a child. I, too, was one who had come from a very strange place in life and was pretty much told that I was nothing and that I would not make it out of high school without having a house full of babies. LOL! I laugh because I really want to add a cuss word right here because for one, even though I may have come from a young mother who didn't finish high school, that did not mean that I wasn't going to finish. I mean, my upbringing was that of being raised civilized, but at the same time, chaotic. Meaning that monstrous word, dysfunction and everything that had come with it, was lurking in the dark alley, waiting on me to sink his teeth in my every emotions, into my being, if you ask me, and ready to tear me apart so that statistically speaking, I would end up like what those who said I would end up, coming from what and where I come from, but indeed, God and Tiffiny! I would not give up, and he, most certainly, did not let go. God meant that thing in his word when he said, "Let your conversation be without covetousness and be content with such things as ye have, for he hath said, 'I will never leave thee, nor forsake thee'" (Hebrews 13:5). (I must admit that I have tried my best to live by this saying.) It's up to us, his children, to believe it. If not, then believe me, I won't fuss! LOL! LOL! LOL! For real! Okay, so back to the story. LOL!

So after I had left my friend, Mr. Gentleman, my one and only true love, my life was as if it was in shambles because I was finally happy in life. I felt like my life was worth living, and I felt that I could go on, be accepted, and loved for the person I was created to be, who was Tiffiny, the little country southern girl from Winnsboro, Louisiana. But I was so naive to life and people at that time especially vindictive people who was right in my family, in which I could not believe. But as I matured in life, I had begun to learn that this happens, and it has happened to many others before my time, during my time, and will continue to happen even after me. I guess that for me, I was blinded by the love I had for family and that they could do no wrong. I remember one time during my counseling session that the counselor told me that one day, I will see the real truth about what I had truly come from and that my friends were so very true! Ugh is what I felt like when the scales had come off. Oh well. Life.

Okay, so as the story goes, my life went down from that point as far as relationships were concerned. I say this because I was so seeking for something in a man that only God could give, which is true inner peace and being content with being in the skin that I was born in. I was running from my past, myself, and then on top of all that, God the creator, all because of me not wanting to deal with myself and not deal with the pain of my past. So I covered the pain by trying to look to someone else, a man, to make me whole.

You know, trying to seek those pleasures of the flesh can be treacherous, especially if a person is not stable mentally or emotionally. What I mean by this is if I had not been an emotional mess, then it would have been okay for me to seek those things of pleasure, which was to obtain and education and career with a nice gentleman, walking beside me, doing those things of my father in heaven so that I could help my fellowman in this life, which was pleasure to me.

Now, I can't speak for others because I think that pleasure is different for everyone whether it be good or bad, or positive or negative. I'm just saying that in my case, since I was not emotionally healthy or mature, I made some really bad choices based off my unhealthiness. I chose abusive relationships. Note, relationships not just one but two, which will lead us to the next chapter.

Chapter 3

<hr/>

Abused and Confused

So I had moved back home to Louisiana from the city life. I no longer had any connections with Mr. Gentleman. My heart was aching, and I had no clue as to which way to go because one thing that I do know was that Mr. Gentleman had my best interest at heart, and he wanted to see me make something of myself, in which he was willing to help me find my way. You got to remember that I was young about nineteen or twenty at that time, sheltered, and I had no clue about life as well as abused, and self-esteem was past being low. So I looked to Mr. Gentleman as a tool to help me find myself, in which was a good thing because for me, coming where I had come from, I needed some kindness, love, and support in order for to go on to college and graduate, in which I did not do until I was broke, busted, and disgusted and had been to hell on earth a couple of times and back. Yeah, I said it: a couple of times. Not just one time. That will come later in the reading. But for now, let's just stick to chapter 3 of my life.

You know, it could have turned out really worse for me. It could have been someone with the wrong intentions toward me, but all I can say is that God was really covering me then, and I did not even realize it until now. You see, I was so downtrodden to the point to where I did not believe that God really cared about me. Well, for one, I had come through an abusive environment, sexually, mentally, physically, verbally, and emotionally until I did not think that anything good could or would ever happen to me and for me. But in spite of where I was during that point of my life, he covered me. Somebody must have been praying for me. So that's why I say this. (Pause. Father, thank you for keeping a sista like me.)

So I moved back home, and I tried to fit into my family's world again, the world that almost destroyed me mentally and emotionally. I had no job, half of an education, no money, and most of all, no Mr. Gentleman. That was enough to just end it all, so I thought at one point. So I held on a little while longer, and I tried to cope the best way that I could, meaning by however and whatever I felt like doing during that point of my life due to the mind-set I was in, which was the mind-set of a victim. That really just made matters worse.

I did not come from a place to where the support was positive. It was more of if you screw up you, are on your on, and you deal with it on your own. Well, I get the tough love thing. I do, but what I do not get is if you sometimes fall short, then sometimes, you need a pick me up. Not a carry me up, but a pick me up. So I did the best I could. I moved from place to place because my mother would not let me live there in peace, and no, I had no one else that felt I could go to in this situation. (But God!) My mother was literally disgusted with me. Nothing I did, good or bad, pleased her. If I did not have anything to give her, then I was just crap out of luck if there was ever such a thing. (This is raw, huh? Welcome to my world.)

Anyway, I was from place to place trying to get back in school, still trying to pursue something that I had no idea that I would ever pursue because of me literally being from place to place, and then, oh yeah, I had had my first child. Oh my goodness. Why did I go and do a thing such as that? Well, for one, I had no education on how not to get one. I mean, I am not blaming anyone. I'm just saying. What's a girl to do when she grew up sheltered and not knowing anything about life? I had limited social skills, no friends, and no one to really teach about life. All I knew was home, school, and church.

I was about twenty-three when I had my first child. So I ended up in a relationship that she approved of, and guess what? He was very, very abusive. Can you believe that? When I told her about my happiness with Mr. Gentleman and that he wanted to help me finish school and to help me make something out of my life, she immediately said, "Move home. Now!" And then I met this wild and crazy man. She was all for it. Yes, he was a provider, just like the man she married, but he was also abusive, just like the man she married.

Yes, abuse did occur in my home for years. I ought to know because I lived the life with them. Now, whether my daddy was provoked into doing the things he did with my momma, I don't know. But I do remember how they would fight a lot, and how at one time, he was the nicest and sweetest dad in the world to me until one day, the daddy-daughter relationship was no more. It was as if he turned completely sour toward me. He used to take me with him sometimes to my grandmother's, and when he would work in his shop cutting wood to make such things as cabinets and picnic tables, I would be there. (He was a carpenter.) It was like a relationship out of this world until that was no more.

I think that I was about in the fifth or sixth grade when my daddy had stopped coming around. I mean, yeah, he and my mother were married, and they still are today, but for about ten to eleven years, I did not see him much. My heart was saddened and broken once again. I am not sure as to why I had so many losses at such a young age, but somebody up above had to be watching out for me because my state of mind should have been far worse than it is today. LOL! Literally!

I ended up in a really bad relationship, and by that time (my age 23), my daddy had moved back home. So they both liked him. But what they did not know was that he was putting his hands on me. He would choke me, drag me outside in front of people on the ground by my shirt, have other girlfriends, threaten me, punch me in the face with his face, and once he I was six months pregnant with his child, he picked me up and slammed me on my back while I was pregnant with his child at my mother's house. I ran to reach for the phone to call the police because my mother was standing there, and she wouldn't do anything. Instead, she grabbed the phone from me, and she pushed me into one of the bedrooms and held the door so I wouldn't get out or something. I don't quite remember exactly about that part because I was so upset, and I remember trying to get out the room and I couldn't get out. Now, ain't that's something? (That's some *sh*——, ain't it?)

That relationship went on like that for about two years until I got tired, and I had enough of being a punching bag. Even when I had left him, he still would follow me around town and harass me as if he owned me. It was as if I had to bow down to him and serve him as if he was the creator! This man literally wanted to suck the very air I breathed from me, and it seemed as if my family didn't care. They laughed about it and thought it was cute. I guess because this was how my parents carried on, and I guess that they felt that I needed some sense beat into me because I refused to be treated like a stray dog or something and because I refused to just be treated as such. I had enough balls to stand up and fight for myself because something inside me knew that this was not right and that this is not how a family supposed to be.

But this was my life, and I had to come to grips and figure out that enough of this craziness was enough and that if I don't get myself together, I may just end up being a lost cause with no point of return in my psyche! So I finally finished nursing school, and I moved out of state again from my own home. I was so eager to leave to the point to where after I took the nurse's state board test. I didn't even wait to see if I passed the test or not. I was just ready to leave my hometown so that I could move on with my life.

Well, lo and behold, while I was running from a negative environment, I ended right back up running into the arms of something that I thought I was done with, which was another abusive relationship! You would have thought that after all that I've been through so far that I would have a new and different mind-set, but I did not. Just because a person left a situation or an environment, it does not mean that the environment left that person!

The reason why I ended up back in another abusive relationship was because I was emotionally unstable. I never did take the time for myself to heal from all the toxic waste for my mental health. I needed a mental detox! So that's why I made the choice I did. I was desperate, needy, insecure, and looking for something that this man could not give me, which was wholeness. (It was not until years later that I realized the only one who could make me whole was/is Jesus himself.)

After I got tired of walking on egg shells, getting threatened with a gun, almost being pushed out of a car on the highway, and hit and slapped while I was pregnant, I said that this is enough, and I made up in my mind that if I did not leave, that somebody was going to probably end up dead.

So I lay down in bed one night while laying on my right side, facing the wall. I said a prayer and asked God that if he made a way for me to leave, then I would and that I would never make a choice like this again, and God did make a way for me, but it was up to me to move on my faith. I had a choice to make in order for me to live and not die. I ended up going to a domestic violence shelter in hopes of me, trying to be safe so that I can stand on my own and live a life free from violence, in which I was no stranger to.

Chapter 4

<hr>

Standing on My Own

Living in a domestic violence shelter was something that I never anticipated. I can remember when I had gone to court to finalize everything, and I remember the judge asking me a question about did I know I was in abuse or something. (I can't really remember her exact words/paraphrasing.) And I said, "Well, it's not like I moved here from another state to get beat up." So I said that to say this, "Abuse was not something I welcomed." I mean, you would think that coming from an environment such as this, I would know the signs, but I didn't. Chaos was normal for me, even though I felt that something wasn't right deep down inside about this relationship, but I held on as much as I could just to be accepted, even if it meant me being treated as if I was nothing. I guess that I was a victim of my circumstances, huh? At this point of my life, I needed some love and affection, and I reached out and grabbed it no matter the cost. (But I do thank God that he let me live to tell you my story!)

So I lived at the shelter for about two years. It wasn't easy. I was all alone (so I thought). I didn't have anyone to help me through this process, but the people who worked for the organization and a few ladies from nearby churches would come by and have a Bible study and prayer with us women. There were also those beautiful souls who would come by and bring donations for us and that was nice, but other than that, I had no family or anyone to help encourage me along the way. I was lost, confused, broke, and not knowing what the next day was going to bring. I held on tight to what I knew best and that was my faith and belief in God. This was the beginning of me turning back to the one I learned about in my youth and that is Jesus Christ, our Lord and savior!

This was the beginning of me learning what it was to have faith, stepping out on it, and standing on it. And that I did, and I am still to this day. This was where I learned to start dealing with my baggage. This was where I started getting counseling. I say this because this was a part of the program. I mean, I didn't want to go to the counseling sessions because I felt like the counselor didn't know me, and she sure didn't have a clue on what it was to come from what I had come from. So I held back on the information that I gave because I didn't feel comfortable enough with her to share my true feelings. I didn't understand it, and anyway, black people don't get counseling. We just deal with whatever, keep going, pray about it, and hope that one day, life changes for the better. But, boy, was I wrong. Well, I have to speak for myself. Well, it wasn't until I met this really clean-shaven, talk, dark, and nice-looking brother when I finally decided to get myself some counseling. (I will tell you about that relationship in the next chapter.)

When I did get counseling, I felt a whole lot better. It was as if a weight was lifted off me. It was as if the word liberation was waiting on me. This was one of the best choices that I could have ever made. I learned to love me for me. I learned to say no. I learned to stand up for myself in a mature way rather than just letting somebody have it without understanding what a person really meant instead of just going off on people for no reason at all because I had issues. I mean, sometimes those who would criticize me were wrong at times, but it was the way I went about letting them know. I mean, I still am growing along with others on this journey, but as for me, my thoughts had become a little clearer, and I could sit outside and enjoy the cool breeze whenever there was one. I could sit outside and look up in the sky while the sun was beaming on my brown skin and smile just because, freely and mentally. LOL!

The reason why I said this was because when I first entered into the counseling session, the counselor asked me what I wanted from this process. And I said all I want to do is smile from within, and to my surprise, I smiled just because. And yes, I worked hard, and I am still working hard to smile just because. Now that is priceless.

I learned to do as the Apostle Paul said in the Bible. Philippians 4:11. "Not that I speak in respect of want, for I have learned, in whatsoever state I am, therewith to be content." No, I don't always live by this because there are those days to where my money gets funny, and I tend to wonder which way is up and which is down. But then, after I have my pity party, I then come to myself, take a look around, and look back over my life and say, "Father, thank you that me and my boys are doing okay with your help." So for me, I have to learn to continue to be grateful and thankful because things could be worse. It's the little things that counts when life throws a bag of lemons at you. Meaning, yes, make lemon and water if you don't have the sugar.

Anyway, that's what many people are doing today! LOL! Besides, it's healthier than all that sugar anyway! So in so, many words just make the best of what you have because life is going to happen, and if we learn the know-how while we are in the valley low, then I think that many people, including myself, can live each day our father in heaven gives us with a smile, just as I learned to do when situations arise.

So being in the homeless shelter did have it advantages as well as the disadvantages, in which I will not harp on because sometimes, you have to take the good with the bad in spite of. Keep your focus, hold your head up, smile, and always, always keep a good outlook on life no matter what situation you to tend to find yourself, in which sometimes is so very hard to do at time, but if you look up and smile, you will get through those situations that life tend to throw at you.

So I made it through the domestic violence process with only help from the good Lord and whatever services that was there while going through the process and that's it. It was lonely and hard at times being a single mother with four boys with limited income, but my father in heaven saw me through, and I was making it. (I'm smiling.)

Chapter 5

Single and on My Own

Well, I manage to stay on top of water with four little boys and no one to help me. Not that I was looking for any help because I was raised to never look to no one for help but to trust God and to help yourself, and I must say that I have tried my best to live those principles my mother taught me. You know, she also taught me that nobody owes you anything, and you owe nobody anything but love and respect and to work hard for what you want. Well, I did until life happened once again. Keep reading. You will see.

So yes, I was able to get my credit straight and buy my first home all on my own with my father's help. Yes, praise him! I had a place of my own, finally, for me and my four boys at that time. It was *so* peaceful and lonely. I mean, I'm just being honest. Even though I had accomplished something that I really didn't think I could. I did what I was taught, I went to church every Sunday, paid my tithes (which this is another story tithing, that is), and I stayed at home and raised my boys. There was still something missing in my life. I used to hear people say that when you feel lonely and empty, you are missing that relationship with God. Well, during those times, I didn't care because I was in a me mode, meaning trying to figure me out, and for someone to say you need a relationship with God was like, yeah, whatever because I was still searching for something because I was lost and whatever they were talking about didn't mean nothing to me then. I was empty, lost, lonely, desperate, clingy, needy, and whatever else you can think of. LOL!

And the sad thing about it was that I didn't care. One reason was because I was grown and on my own and doing my own thing and that was being dysfunctional, that is. In my mind, as long as I wasn't hurting anyone, then what difference did it make? Because after all, it was my life, and the way I saw it then was nobody gave a damn, and if I lived to see the next day, then oh well. But there were those times in my life to where I was hoping that I didn't die because I didn't want to leave this earth with my business not straight, meaning I have not completed my assignment here on earth, I was taught was to serve God and serve others, meaning help my fellow human brothers and sisters along this journey called life no matter their creed or color.

I have to say that even though I had come up through a mess, the good Lord still blessed me to grow up in a place where the women were as real as the word real itself. This is where I learned about humanity and a higher power, and to that, I am grateful. So you see, I have been making lemonade and lemon water all my life! LOL.

I learned at a very early age to make the best of what you have and keep on going. You have to keep pushing, and you have to keep doing good and goodwill follow. Needless to say that I still try my best to live by this, and to my surprise, I see that I have been getting by. Praise God again! Hallelujah! So, yes, I was in my home, still feeling lost and empty. No matter how hard I prayed, and no matter how I gave to the church, my issues were still there. I was an emotional mess! So I kept going with my four boys. I kept pushing, and I kept on hoping that life would turn for me. Well, guess what? It didn't. As a matter of fact, my life had got worse. Keep reading.

It had been about two years that I have been living in my house with my boys, and believe me, it wasn't an easy road, but I had refused to just give up because of those four beautiful little boys who were depending on me. You know, the whole time I was by myself with my boys, they never knew that anything was wrong. They always had a place to sleep, food to eat, and shoes on their feet! LOL! I mean, good shoes at that! They didn't know that there were days that Momma didn't have gas to get back to work sometimes, or that after I paid all my bills, I couldn't buy food for them to eat and that I had to go to this church every month for almost two years to get food to feed them. But I have to say that God always made a way for me and mine. So I know the man for myself. I know that he is real! That is why my book is entitled what it is. I was lost, and now, I am found. Divinely, that is! LOL!

So Momma made it look good. Momma didn't let them see me sweat. She just kept on going penniless with a prayer in her pocket. I can remember the time when I was at work, and the tears started coming down my eyes, wondering how I was going to get back and forth to work that week. And I had got a phone call from a former coworker who used to work with me. The coworker called me one day and said, "I was thinking about you, and I have a fifty-dollar check for you." And, boy, that was all I needed to make until I had gotten paid. Now, isn't God something awesome? I know some may say, "Well, maybe it was a coincidence, or maybe it was just a random call to say, 'Hey, girl, I'm thinking about you.'" But for me, it was my faith!

There were also agencies that I went to for help, and to those people, I was very grateful to them for helping me get through those tough times. You know, as I was going through this time of my life, all I would think about were my boys, and if Momma didn't keep it together, and if Momma faltered, then what? If Momma gave up and called it quits, then what? What would or could happen to them? This was one of my motivators. This was one of the driving forces behind my will to keep on pushing in this life no matter the circumstances.

I sometimes wondered if I had left them with their daddy, what would they be like? How would they turn out? I say this because I have been around mothers who have left their children, and for whatever reason they were left, they just were. Now, I'm passing judgment here, so please try to understand what I am trying to say and where I am going with this.

All I am saying is that seeing this helped me be the mother I am today. Yes, I am overprotected, but can you blame me? After all, children do not ask to come here, and when we have children, we should try our damnedest to try our best to help them become the best man or woman that they could humanly be. Yes, I have had those times, and I still do, wondering if they will get it together, or if all the hard work I put into my boys will pay off. But I tell myself all I can do is do the best I possibly can by encouraging them and correct them when they are wrong, but most all, loving them no matter what because they are a part of me, and as for me, I feel that I owe them that much.

I can remember one day I said a prayer. I said, "Father, I know that I did not make all of the right choices having my children [meaning me and the father could not get it together to raise them], so I'm asking you to please help me." I also told him I accept my responsibility as a mother, and all I need is for you to help me because I made these choices, and it is nobody's fault but my own. And from there, I went on in faith, raising and loving the best part of me, which were and are my boys.

You know, I have had people tell me that I was overprotecting my boys and that my boys were Momma's boys. You know, I really never cared about any of that because what I have found out was this: somebody will always have something to say no matter what you do, and in this case, all I was simply trying to do was to be a mother and teach my boys about life and that whatever choices you make in life, good or bad will follow you, so just take the good route. I also told them that life will happen, but you have to be strong-minded, watch the company you keep, and always, always have a prayer in your pocket with your head held high trusting in God, our father, to help you get through this life. And also, help your fellow man (as I was told) no matter their status, economic situation, or color. I taught my boys to always stand up for what's right and never back down from a fight no matter and to stand your ground as a man. I just simply taught my boys to be real and try to get along with others who may not want to get along with you.

You know, as I was raising my boys, at one point in my life, I really thought that I was so strong and tough and that I didn't need a man to help me raise my boys. "Oh, I can do this all by myself." But as these boys started getting up and growing, I started to realize, boy, was I wrong! I started to realize that a woman cannot teach a man to be a man, but she dog on sure can come close to teaching them when she is all she have if she doesn't give up and give in and not let men or other people come in try to destroy them or kill their spirit, in which will be my next chapter.

Chapter 6

In Love Again; so I thought

What will today hold for me? What will work be like today? Work is just work. People come, people go. One day, I was sitting in my office at work, patiently waiting for the day to go by, talking to my coworker, and laughing and joking around because that day in the immunization clinic was a very slow one. So here comes this somewhat-dark skin, nice height, and neatly groomed brother, walking into the office where me and my coworker was in with a smile, offering me a piece of gum.

I said, "A piece of gum?" I said, "Why not get me lunch or something?"

And to my surprise, he said, "What do you want?"

I said, "I want a combo."

I said this because our lunch breaks were only thirty minutes, and there weren't too many places that we could go to get lunch. There was this fast-food Asian restaurant across the street, and he would go there all the time. And to my surprise, he went and got it for me! Whoa! How about them peaches, plums, and pears? (My southern language. LOL.)

So I guess he thought that he did something because he had kept coming back, but the next time, he had come back to my office and tried to make conversation with me. The nerve of this brother! Okay, okay, wait a minute. I know what some of you may be thinking! Why not? You got four boys, and here comes this man who's kind of interested in you, and you're acting up like this. Well, I had reasons. I had children to protect, and besides, I had just come out of an abusive relationship right before I started working at the immunization clinic, and I did not want any drama, nor did I want to bring craziness around my boys because I didn't move to Texas just because. I had goals in mind, and I was going to reach them. So, no, I did not have time for no more of the dysfunctional drama. I did not care if it was a man, woman, boy, or girl. I just needed some sense of normalcy in my life for me and my boys, but let the truth be told, I was an emotional mess! Even though I was good or responsible in many areas in my life, I was struggling with that area of when it had come to relationships. Now, when I did get into something that was not right, such as an unhealthy relationship, you best believe I was getting out of it! But this brother appeared to be somewhat different. He was altogether mentally and emotionally. (Well, so I thought.)

When he respectfully walked into my office one day, and he stood in the doorway, I said, "What do you want?" I just went straight to the point! I said, "What do you want from me? I am a single mother with four boys, and I don't have time to date. *So* you might as well move around." But nevertheless, he kept pursuing me.

One reason he kept walking to my office was because he worked there at the clinic. He was a security officer, and he had told me he had been watching me for a year and thought that I was cute. He said I was a little mean, but he thought I was really cute and that loving me would be beautiful! I was like, wow, I was taken! LOL! No, don't go there. It wasn't like that. Just because he said something nice that day didn't mean that I just dropped and fell to his knees or something. But what he said stuck with me. I didn't have anything like that since Mr. Gentleman.

Oh, before I forget, that was one of the reasons why I went to Dallas in the first place: to try to find Mr. Gentleman because I thought he was there because that was the last place I left him at. The second time we got back together, he looked me in my eyes, and he said to me, "You have to do this, this time. You have to finish nursing school. You go on back home and finish, and we will meet back up here." With tears in his eyes, he said, "She's leaving me again."

I said, "I'll come back once I finish."

After a few visits, it was as if he disappeared. The calls stopped coming, and I was in school, trying to fight to stay in because for one, nursing school was not easy. But by God's grace and mercy, I graduated, and there was no more Mr. Gentleman. So I had to push that thought back far away from my mind and think about my little boys because I made the choice to bring them into this world, and I had to try to get my mind right in order to try to raise them the best way I knew how as I mentioned before.

So needless to say that the security officer, too, had game. He, too, was up to something. I couldn't see it at first then, but now as I look back over it, he, too, had issues. But we got together and tried it. I was like, well, I might as well. I have all these kids, and there aren't too many men who would want to come in and help raise other people's children, so I let go a little. Just a little.

We dated for about a two years. The first year was okay. I mean, I was still trying to put it together because I have these boys, and I wasn't going to let nobody come in and kill their little spirits. You see, when a person a lot of times has been broken down, and they feel like they can't go on, sometimes the spirit has been broken. And when this happens, this can tend to stop one from accomplishing almost anything in life. And believe me, I wasn't going to be one of those black mommas to let that happen if I could help it because children are innocent, and God put them in our lives to take care of them as he said in his word about children being a gift. They are, it's just that some people don't realize it.

So anyway, I let this brother come into our lives, letting him know of the situation and that I had issues, and if he wanted to be with me, then it was up to him. I mean, what more can you do when a person lets you know straight up that you have stuff going on inside you and that you had just come through abuse and that you are not going to take any mess from nobody anymore but all at the same time being willing to try to work with someone to have a future together? I was willing to try with him and be his girl, love him, and be good to him even though so much had happened to me, and I was misused and abused. I was still willing to put all that behind me and try with him.

You know, you have those who bring baggage with them and take it out on others because of what somebody else did to them. Well, that wasn't the case with me. I just always thought that it's not fair to the new person you meet because they didn't cause the heartaches and pain. Why make them suffer for what happened to you in your past? I mean, yeah, I know what it's like, but I also know what it's like to let it go and try to live free with that person. My problem was that I would always end up with the wrong person. Okay, so I got with Mr. Security Officer, and everything was going good. He would come by and visit me and the boys, and he would take time out with my baby. And that's what got me. I was like, wait a minute. Whoa! I had a four-month-old baby, and this brother was taking care of him like he was his own baby. And that right there was what stole my heart. I gave in an inch more.

Everything was going okay. I mean, he wasn't no Mr. Gentleman, but I was willing to put all that behind me and start fresh with a brother. And besides, I had really started liking him a lot. But there was something going with him that didn't add up. Remember when he first had come to talk to me in my office? I forgot to mention this. I asked him if was he single, or was he married, or in a relationship, and he boldly said, "No. I have been single for a year now, and it's just me." And so I really found that hard to believe because the brother was nice looking to me, he smelled nice, he had on a uniform, and he was employed. "Really? Come on now. You are not seeing somebody?"

But he denied it to the end until one day, my son said, "Momma, how come he never invites us over?" And my eldest at that time was in the fifth grade, I think. And I was like, "Well, he said that he has this roommate [a guy] who parties a lot and that he didn't want to bring us around that type environment." My son said, "So he still can take us to his house?" And you know, he had a point. But I didn't put up a fight or an argument because I was not and still not the argument type. I mean, I can go there with you and dance a jig or two, but for what? It wasn't worth it. But when I found out the truth, I went off! Because I felt like he deceived me. All he had to do was to be straight with me. I was straight with him, and anybody who knows me knows that what you see with Tiffiny is what you get.

But anyway, I found out that this clean-shaven, well-groomed employed brother had a whole other family. Yes, a wife. Can you believe that? I bet some of you are saying, yes, we can. LOL! Well, there were two reasons why I went off. One was because when I first got with him, I told him, "I can handle almost anything but not you being deceitful with me. Just be straight up with me, and I can respect you more." If the brother had told me that he was separated, working on a divorce, and trying to get things together, that would have been better. I would have stepped back and let him figure out what he wanted to do, but *no*, he insisted on being with me, so he said. And second, my mother always told us girls to never ever talk to a married man because nothing good will come to you and to never ever destroy homes. Yeah, she told us girls that because we saw firsthand of what it was like to have women come in and try to destroy another woman's home. And when she told me that I said that I would never ever do something like this if I can help it because there are others involved and that's something I never wanted on my consciousness. But lo and behold, I ended up with the brother. But wait, let me tell you what happened.

He called me one day from a number that I didn't recognize. (Caller ID was something else.) So I looked at the number, and I wondered, *What in the world?* He told me he was at his neighbor's house, using their phone and that he couldn't stay on the phone long. Yes, I bought into it, but when I looked at the name on the caller ID, the name was a regular name. But he told me his neighbors were Hispanic and that didn't set well with me. So one day, I waited to call when I knew he wasn't in, and this sister answered the phone.

And I said, "Who is this?"

And she said, "I am his wife."

Wife! I said, "His wife? He told me he wasn't married."

I hung up, and I waited for him to call me. And I asked him why he lied to me. I said, "I told you not to be deceitful to me." And I told him, "Stay away from me and don't call me no more." Well, two weeks had passed, and by that time, I had been talking to him for a year, and I had missed being around him. He had got me. He sucked me in like a sponge, soaking up water. But I was not going to go against what I was taught about, breaking up people's home no matter if they were working things out or not. I didn't care. Just don't come my way with your drama.

But for two weeks, he called and called and left messages on my phone, saying, "This is not what you think," and "We are separated," and "We are getting a divorce." Well, I gave in.

And I said, "Okay. If this is true, then go on and do what you have to do and then we will talk."

But he said no. So he finally convinced me to come over so he can talk to me, and we talked. He said, "Let's move in together, and I will work on getting the divorce." I was like at first, no, but he made it sound so good until I was like okay. But he told me that they were not together and that they had been separated for a year and that he wanted to be with me.

By that time, I was really struggling with four boys, and I made the choice based on me needing help with my boys. And besides, he was pretty decent. He would help me take my boys to and from day care, and he helped with my four-month-old. So I said, "Okay, but you have to go through with your divorce if that's what you are going to do. And if not, just go on your way."

So we got together. After two years of dating, we got married. I think that since I was alone, a single mother, and no family out here to help me, I was desperate, and I made the choice to get with him. If I tell you that I should have waited, I should have because for twelve years, the relationship was pure *hell!* We argued, argued, argued. We never saw eye to eye. And another thing. Remember when I told you he had issues? Well, he did, but he told me I needed counseling and that I did. I went. I got counseling because I was trying to do things right, and I was trying to get along with him and to learn how to be stable with a guy for a change.

After Mr. Gentleman, I would only be in a relationship for about two years and then I was gone. If it was something I didn't like, then I was out. But when you are in relationship, you have to learn how to compromise, and you have to learn how to agree to disagree. I think you know what I mean. I won't get into that, but that was some of the reasons as to why I went to get counseling because I knew that I had to grow up someday and that my boys needed to see what it was to learn what it was to be a man. But, boy, was I wrong again. I had the right plan, but the wrong man.

No, he wasn't abusive in the sense to where he would hit me or us because that I wasn't having that. The problem that I had with this brother was that he never respected me from the beginning, and if a man or a woman gets into a relationship, and they have no respect for each other, then they surely are not going to respect what they have and in this situation my boys. When there's no respect, then there is no love because love is respect! But I stayed, thinking if I go to counseling, and if I take him to church, then he will be the ideal man. Well, I was wrong because for one, he never had the right motives toward me anyway. He was just using me to get back at his wife for cheating on him, and I was just caught up in my feelings, thinking that this brother loved me and my boys, and he wanted to be with me, but he didn't because his actions showed.

His mind was across town. I couldn't understand that then because I was into myself and in the heat of the moment, but throughout the relationship, I saw that I was something out of convenience. I was a young hardworking nurse, trying to get my life on track. I kept my house nice, neat, and clean, and he saw that. But his intentions were never to get with me, so I believe that he saw the difference in me and her, and he chose me because of how I was able to keep things together even though I was struggling financially.

So life went on, and as I mentioned previously, I did get counseling. And again, that was one of the best choices that I could have ever made. I had begun to look at life in a different eye versus me looking at life with a chip on my shoulders. I learned and I am still learning how to look at others in a different way instead of just looking at them in my own eyes, which were distorted and unclear.

There are reasons why people do what they do. We just have try to come to an understanding by communicating with each other and also by trying to be as honest as we can to each in love and respect especially if there are others involved in your life. I know not everyone will and can do this, but at least if you try, then you will some type direction to go in your relationship and which way to go in life instead of always being stuck. Sometimes the answers lie within us on some of our issues that we may be having. We just have to dig deep and look at it for what it really is and either move on or fix it.

Through our ups and downs in this marriage, I learned something from this, and I'm pretty sure that he learned something from me too. I have to speak for myself, and even though this relationship was built on a lie, and I would not do this again, I learned from this man on how to communicate effectively. I learned to listen, I learned how to be stable, to not go back and forth when it comes to my feelings, and to not always go on my feelings. I mean, he was no gentleman, but I did get the message. Through all the arguing and fussing, I learned how to be still a little bit and not to just assume something when it comes to people and to not just go off what I think because half of the time, what we may be thinking could be something totally different. I learned from him to just take life as it is and to not panic about situations when they happen. I mean, I am about 90 percent now when it comes to having panic attacks or anxiety, and to him, I owe that, too, because like I mentioned, it was no walk in the park with him as far as him explaining things to me. He was pretty rough with me, but that was because he had issues himself and also because he was a lot older than me, and he was on a whole other level when it had come to maturity in that aspect of the relationship. I had no clue on what it was to communicate my feelings or how I felt. So I am very grateful to him for that.

Yes, I could go on and bash him, but I choose not to because there were some other things that have happened to make a sister cringe, but I was trying to hang in there and learn how to be a stable-minded individual because emotionally, I was all over the place.

And as far as my boys go in the relationship, there was never just any father-son interaction because he was so set on discipline until he didn't relate to them. Or maybe it was because I didn't let him get close to them. Or maybe it was because I felt as though maybe he wasn't showing me enough of himself to let me know that he wanted the best for me and my boys. Just know this that my boys were not harmed, and they were safe because if not, I would not be here, writing my life story! LOL! LOL! For real! For real!

This was a relationship that could have possibly worked, but when you have one person letting go and doing all the bending, and the other one is holding back, then there will be some issues. I mean, okay, yes, I think you should hold back some in beginning of the relationship because of you learning about the person and trying to get to know them, but when you say I do, and when you say, "Okay, let's do this," and "I love you," then their actions should show it. But whatever and however I did it, I tried it, and needless to say that the relationship did not work all because his motives were not right from the beginning. Lesson was well bought and paid for on my end.

You know, when I was in this relationship, I learned how valuable the presence of the male figure. A man can either make their family or break them. What I mean by this is that no matter how of a mother you are to your child, whether you are raising a boy or a girl, there is something about that male presence. There is something about a man that helps to get the message across to a child so that they can either go out in the world and build it up or tear it down. It's just that crucial! I saw this while I was in this relationship, trying to do the best I could with a blended family. I have to say that if I had not been the mother that I am, I think that the outcome of my boys would that of something probably unimaginable. I'm not quite sure, but I don't think that they would have finished high school.

So what I am trying to say is this: when you have a child or children, it is our responsibility as parents to do our best to try to raise them as best we can, and if you don't know, then I advise you to get involved with such programs that the schools or that your community may have to help your child be all that he/she can be in a positive manner and also utilize counseling services in your area.

And always, always say a prayer for covering over your children because what I have found out for myself is this: no matter how far you may have think you have gone, when it comes past the point of no return with your children when trying to raise them whether you made good or bad choices when trying to keep a roof over their head, God will keep you and your children if you do what's right by them, which is trying to be the best parent you possibly can humanely with love, that is.

And then this is where you will see your hard work pay off. No, it's not easy, but when you love your children and treat them with respect and try to give them what they need along this journey to make it out here in this jungle, then you've pretty much beat the odds of them not turning out to be nothing. But instead, they will take what you have given them and strive toward something greater than you probably could ever imagine in their life!

I really had to go there because of the love and passion I have for my boys. I made the choice to have them no matter if they had or have a father in their life. I felt that it was crucial for me as a mother to keep on going and to fight for them to have a pretty decent life. I refused to let a man or just some man come in and mistreat them because of something that he was hung up on or just because he had past issues with someone or something in his childhood and then bring that to my dinner table. I mean, please don't get me wrong. My heart goes out to those brothers who have had a rough start in life, and they have my sympathy. But there comes a time in one's life to where a person has to rise up behind all the mishaps, the setbacks, the hurt, the pain, the abuse, the rape, and the rejection. And oh, did I mention the mistreatment from the church people? (Yeah, them too.) Work through those issues so that you can be all that you can be and give to others something that is beautiful and fulfilling, which is life full of love and laughter.

I got that, but I was not having it. I just wasn't. Needless to say, this relationship was a dud. I stayed in the relationship, trying to figure him out and me out while all at the same time trying to play my role as a mother and wife with what I had inside me. I was broken inside. I was an emotional wreck. But no matter how emotional I was, I kept my boys close to me, loving them and taking care of them, making sure that nobody would try to hurt them because they are a part of me. And when someone such as a child is a part of you, what do you do? You love them, and you take care of them. And that's all I was ever trying to do. I took care of my responsibilities because I made the choice to have my boys the way I did. I mean, I wasn't educated on protecting myself on how not to have children until I was ready financially or emotionally to take care of a child, nor did I have any good examples on what it was to look for in a man, so I did what I knew and that was to protect, nurture, and love my babies because they are mine no matter what!

Before I move on to the next part of my life story, I would like to talk to an audience of those parents who are raising their children. As you may see, when it comes to children, this is something I don't take lightly. I would like to say to you, the young mothers and fathers raising your children. Stop having these babies and not taking care of them. We owe it to them. Stop letting people mistreat them. And to those who are mistreating them, stop mistreating them because according to the Bible, children are a gift from God. And what do you do with a gift? You open the package with care and take care of what's inside. Meaning if we bring another being into this world, it is our responsibility to try our damnedest to make sure that we teach them good things, treat them with respect for themselves, and their fellowman, but most of all, try your best to respect God up above. That's if you believe in such a power as the most high! (LOL. No offense, and I sure hope none were taken. I'm coming from a place of sincerity and love. That's all.)

I said all this because it saddens my heart to see all these babies and children being hurt, killed, and suffered all because of choices being made to do so. And until we as a human race get it together, then things in this world will continue to get worse. And after all, the youth of today are our future, and if we don't stop the madness, there will be the weak and helpless at hand of their mercy, which right now it looks scary!

So I am not the perfect mother, nor do I carry myself as so, but what I do know is that if you use what I say, then your life as far as children goes will be a lot better. And if you show them love and kindness and balance, the child-to-parent relationship out I think that you will indeed be well pleased with the outcome even though there will those times where you will scratch your head and wonder, *Should I just run away or stay?* Because I sometimes still do, but I am in it to win it! (I'm laughing.) And besides, what you give out is sure to return whether good or bad. (Holy Bible.)

Now, back to this relationship and what happened after. I helped nurse this man back to health all by myself on a walker six months pregnant and in pain after being ejected from a moving vehicle which is Chapter 7.

Chapter 7

So I Thought It Was Love: The Car Accident

So me and Mr. Man were married now for about two months. Yes, now my life was on point! I'm married, I have a pretty-okay job, I got a man who was working, and yes, it was on. Finally! Well, okay, to be real with you, the relationship was not all that because for one, I never felt a true connection. I mean, his body was there with me, but his mind was not there with me. I mean, he said it was, and he talked a good game after the fact that he was in a whole other relationship, but I believed him lies and all. You know, a person can tell you they love you until the clouds fall out of the sky, but if their actions do not line up with what they are saying, then you know it's time to do something a little different. Now wait a minute. I do believe that some people can change and that some people can learn to love, but there are those who keep telling you this and that, and when it really comes down to it, you will see what love is. I'll show you. Keep reading.

So I bought the lines. He said, "I love children, I'm active with children, and I like to teach them things. And since you have boys,

I will take them to their practice and games, or I will be involved with them when it comes to sports." And I was like, "Okay. I can let you do that." But what I had begun to see was something different. I mean, he did take them to practice, he did drop them off in the mornings at school, and he would pick them up, but what I noticed was that he was trying to kill their spirits! *Oh.* Hell no! I am so sorry to put this in here because somebody who is religious may pick this up and read it, but this is the raw and uncut truth here. I'm keeping it real, and I'm telling you like it happened.

What I mean by he was trying to kill their spirits was that he was trying tear them down mentally and emotionally. He said he was trying to teach them to respect him, but *hell* no, not the way he was trying to do it. He was trying to cut them down with words or talk down to them as if they were nothing. And anybody who knows Tiffiny, this right here ain't happening. Not with my boys because I love my boys.

Now, don't get me wrong. I do believe in teaching children to be respectful and to respect others, and I do believe in discipline, but I do not believe in disciplining a child being negative with the discipline, or just literally cutting a child's spirit all the way down to the point until they can't hold their head up to look at the sunlight. (I mean, literally look up at the sky, meaning they will lose all hope.)

I know what that's like, and that is mental torture on a child. And as most of us know, when this happens, the child will grow up and have issues. Now, please don't take this wrong! I'm not saying that they can't be saved, or they can't be helped. It's just that they will have to undergo some construction in their life, and they can really have a tough time trying to figure themselves out, or they may turn to something awful as we can see in our world today. And that was something that was not going to happen.

Well, I stayed with the man, and we talked and talked and talked. And we got counseling. And I got counseling, thinking that he would get better and that out relationship would be off-the-charts perfect. I even had the brother going to church, thinking, *Yeah, this will do it. He will be the man with a plan for me.* But, boy, was I wrong. He just wasn't feeling it. The brother just was not into me.

No matter how hard I worked to try to keep the family together, and no matter how hard I refereed with him and my boys, it was a hit and miss. I'll show you what I mean.

So it was two months now, and we got married. (We dated for about two years.) Shortly after we got married (two months), we were in a really bad car accident. I can remember I was at work on a Friday (six months pregnant), and I was telling a coworker of mine that I really dreaded going home this weekend to my sister's wedding rehearsal. I was supposed to be in the wedding, but I told her I didn't want to because I was getting too big. I'm not exactly sure what happened about me still being in the wedding, but I do remember getting ready to go home to the rehearsal.

So it was a Friday evening that we got on the highway to go to Louisiana. We got into Shreveport, and after we passed a few a couple of towns (estimate—a couple of towns or so), my husband and I stopped to get something to eat, which was about I think around 9:00 p.m. and then we got into our SUV buckled up and headed toward home. Maybe about thirty minutes into the drive, I noticed the truck swerving. I had fallen asleep, and I was awakened by the swerving.

And so I asked my husband at that time, "What's going on?"

And he replied, "I'm trying to get over, but this truck would not let me in."

The truck had pressed on the gas, and he speeded up so that we would not get over and then he slowed down. So my husband waited always on down the road, and he put his signal light on to get over in the left lane on I-20. The guy hit the gas, and he hit us so hard and knocked me and my family off the interstate. I remember going up and screaming and that was it.

The next thing I knew, I woke up, screaming, "I'm hurting!" in the emergency room in Minden, Louisiana. My husband was still in the truck. (After me and the three children were ejected. And, yes, they were buckled up, car seat, and all age appropriate. I always made sure that we would always buckle up. Ages of my three children at that time were seven, six, and two, I think). The truck with my husband still in it had flipped 144 feet while he was still in there, and the guy who had hit us kept going and never did come back, nor did he give a damn about reporting it. I think that they finally found him, but nothing ever came of it. He was never charged, but I guess that's what life is like when your life doesn't matter to some people until it happens to them or someone close to them. And you know what? I never got mad or angry about what happened. I was just glad to be alive. (Life!)

So my husband had to be flown out to the hospital in Shreveport out because his neck was broken, and both his legs were hyper extended all the way back, so he had to have surgery. (What a mighty God I serve! Understatement.) And once my family had made it to the hospital to pick up the three little ones (Oh yes, they made it! God did that thing. Nobody died. Praise God!), I was flown out to the hospital because I was bleeding internally and my liver was lacerated and I had sustained a bad head injury. (Oh, but, God!)

I can remember being in ICU, being hooked up to an IV pole, getting my two units of blood, being in good spirits, and asking the nurses if they would wheel my husband in the room so I could pray for him before surgery. And before they wheeled him off to surgery, they stopped him by my bed and wheeled him close to me and I reached out and grabbed his hand and he reached out and grabbed my hand and I prayed for him that all be well with him and it did. (To God be the glory!)

I can also remember the staff and their joyful spirits and having compassion for us at the LSU hospital in Shreveport, but there was this one doctor that stood out to me. He stood out to me because he had come into my room once I was released from ICU and said, "Can I shake your hand?" I said yeah. And then he said, "You know in an accident like this, nobody ever makes it through and not even the baby makes it through, and your baby is still attached to you!" He said, "But in your case, everybody in your family made it and that is a miracle!" Yes, indeed it was. Why? I don't know, but it was. Maybe it was all those prayers that I sent up from years ago to God to please let me be around to raise my children so that they won't be mistreated, or maybe it was the prayer that I always pray when I travel. Whatever God's reason, he did that thing, and to him, I owe him my life fifty times over. So this is one of the main reasons why I am writing this book: to let others know that no matter your trial or circumstances, there is somebody who really truly cares about you and who loves you too! (LOL.)

So we stayed in the hospital for about two weeks. I stayed a week, learning how to walk again with my baby stuck to me in pain, not knowing what the next day was going to bring. And my husband stayed longer because of his neck surgery and also because of both his legs being hyperextended all the way back. He really had to learn how to walk. He was there mentally, and he could talk, but he could not walk, or he could not feed himself, bathe himself, nor could he clean, or shave himself. It was as if he was a baby all over again, and when I saw that, the love I had for him showed it. I was right there by his side, making sure that he was being taken care of and that he was fed and cleaned. Well, I am a nurse. What do you expect? LOL.

But he, on the other hand, was not into me as I was into him during that time. I believe that his niceness was out of guilt from thinking he caused the accident rather than being from pure love. But that was my husband, and I was going to try my best to keep my end of the vows up for better or for worse and in sickness and in health. And believe me when I tell you, I did that thing.

Right after he was discharged, I had my family to take me to take him to pick him up in my rental. I went back to my family's home and stayed for about a week. I was ambulating on a walker, struggling to walk. I went and picked up my kids from my older two boys' grandmother's house, and I hightailed it back to Dallas, shaking and panicking, driving all the way back all by myself with my two kids, my husband, and my mother (all wearing seat belts, LOL) with my faith and my strength not knowing what I was going to walk into after having the wind completely knocked out of me. The test of time showed.

After I had gotten back to Dallas and gotten my family settled in, I started to wonder to myself how I was going to make it now and how was I going to take care of my family all by myself on a walker, in pain, and six months pregnant. My mother only stayed a week, and all she did was cook. Her husband kept calling her, asking her,

"When are you coming back?" and that "You got a family here, and you need to come home and take care of them." If that wasn't a blow below the belt. Well, I was used to it. I was used to no family helping me, but I felt like I was at the lowest point of my life, and I really needed somebody, but that's the hand that some of us are dealt.

I am writing this part with tears in my eyes because it hurt then when you never asked anybody for anything and when you were always the one giving of your time and resources and to have your own family to treat you as if you never existed is suicidal. Yes, I did, during this time, thought about taking my life not that nobody cared, but then I thought about my boys. What would happen to them? Will they be separated? Will they grow up screwed up in the head? What? So I held on a little longer, I held on to my faith a little tighter, and I prayed a little louder in hopes of my father in heaven would see me through this rough patch in my life, not knowing what the next day was going to bring and not knowing if the pain in my body would go away and not knowing if my memory would hold up to the day-to-day struggles of trying to keep up with remembering to pick up the kids from school, turning the stove off when I cooked, or trying to remember what I was cooking, or even trying to remember my way back home. It was a *s-t-r-u-g-g-l-e*!

But God held me close and tight, and he did not let me go as the songwriter said, "He did that! He did that!" Thank you, Father. Please excuse me if you will, but I have to pause right here because if you knew what I knew, and if you knew that, yes, there is indeed a higher power, you would understand my praise right now. I had to literally get up every day that God allowed me all by myself when my mother had left me all alone on my lonesome.

That week she stayed, I had to drag my left leg while trying to ambulate on a walker, get my boys up for school (four boys), dress them, get them off to school, then come home help my husband get himself together. I had to bathe him, feed him, shave him, dress him, take him to his doctor's appointments, and whatever else that was needed, concerning his daily activities, while again, as I mentioned previously, I myself was on a walker barely able to walk while I was six months pregnant. If this wasn't enough to make a woman want to holler. But I didn't because of the love I had/have inside me for my family.

All I knew was to keep going. All I knew was to fight for the breath I was breathing and to hold on to my faith all the while listening to my disabled grandmother encourage me and tell me, "If you have my blood in you, you will keep on going." She would also, from time to time, send me money and help me and my family to stay hopeful. It was the sweet words of her mouth that soothed my aching heart, and the smile on her face that made it glad. It was her kind spirit that gave me courage to hang on just a little while longer. It was a grandmother's love that gave me the push I needed when I felt like I couldn't go on and the hand of my father in heaven who held me close so that I wouldn't lose it all! It was a divine intervention that says it all! I had to go there because the pain was excruciating. I had to share with you how I made it to this point of my life. This was when I found out what love really was and is, which brings me to my husband and that he was not feeling a sista.

So earlier when I mentioned about my husband and him not feeling me when life happened to us, I really saw who he was when trouble came knocking. I saw how the love I thought he had for me was not there. Although I did my wifely duties for him during this time and was nursing him back to health, while I was carrying his child, walking on a walker in pain, he had the nerves to say, "She don't care about me." Can y'all believe that? This dude was asking about another woman while he was in my care! Okay, I know you are lost. Let me explain to you what I mean by this.

I drove him to pick his son up, and when we picked his son up, he got back in the car and said, "She don't care about me." Well, for one, I didn't and couldn't say anything because shock went through my body in disbelief because first of all, I was his wife; and second, because I was in pain, trying to hold things together, six months pregnant, just got thrown from a moving vehicle, taking care of him, and this is what came out of his damn mouth? I know it. I know it, and I am sorry I went there. I had a moment. I couldn't believe what I was hearing after all that I was doing for him. That just showed me how he truly felt and that he really didn't love me.

Well, I guess that I had that coming because remember way back in the story I shared with you as to how we had met and what happened about how I found out that he was married and he lied to me about it and all that good stuff? He was still in love with her, and I didn't even know it until that day. I just went on letting him tell me that he wanted to be with me and how we should be as a family and that he was ready to be a father to my boys and all that too. But his actions, as far as loving me, showed something different. But since we were married, and I said I do, and I did! So I kept going, I kept pushing, I kept crying, and I kept on praying in hopes of God turning things around in my life for the better. Well, I bet some of you are wondering, *Did it turn around? Did it?* No, it didn't. As a matter of fact, things in my life got *w-o-r-s-e*! Stay with me. I'll tell you in the next chapter.

Chapter 8

Homeless Once Again: How I Lost It All and Almost My Mind!

It was four years after the car accident, and I was still holding on by a string. No job, no one to help me when I felt like I needed help, no money in the bank, and no nothing. I was just out in the ocean, drifting in hopes of a ship to come by and save me from going under. No life jacket, no little boat, or big boat, for that matter, no canoe, just me, my grandmother's love, and my faith in God is all I had to get through the turbulence in my life at that point of my life.

And you know, as I look back, it was a powerful support group! I was still unable to work due to the head injury I had and due to chronic pain, going through my body. So I continued to try to keep my mind focused on the on things in life while at same time, wondering how I was going to make it. If I tell you my father in heaven always made sure that me and my boys always had a roof over our heads and food to eat. I think for me that this trial that happened to me was a wake-up call.

What I mean by this is all my life, I was taught to go get it whether it be a college degree, house, car, money in the bank, or getting a business. My mother pushed me to the point to where I was always trying to do something by working hard and by having pride in working hard. So for me, when this happened to me, I was clueless as to how I was going to function because all I knew was to work and to hold my own. But what do you do when you can't go out and get it? What do you do when your health fails you, and you have not a soul to help you? What do you do when you are sick in your body, and you have to try to muscle up the strength from somewhere just to get up and wash your face with no help from no one? What do you do? Well, fight. Sometimes that word for me was unreal, being that fight was what I came from. But when the boat tips over in the deep blue sea, what do you do? It was either sink or swim. And my friend, to my surprise, I was able to stay on top water, fighting for my life.

You know, I used to hear people say things like, "God is good," and "Why doubt God?" Or they would say my faith was up and down. For what? Well, I argue that because when you are thrown out in a body of water, the ocean, with nothing and not a sight of land nowhere, then what? No, I did not have faith strongly as one would when they are surrounded by a great support system. Yes, my faith was up and down when all I had was my disabled grandmother, calling me day in and day out, telling me, "Tiffiny, you got to hold on. You got children. You got to keep pushing and not give up." And for the life of me, I was at that point of just giving up the breath I was breathing. After all, my life didn't matter. Who cared about a woman with five boys, trying to make it? Who cared? Well, I will tell you who cared. My father above and my dearly sweet grandmother.

Okay, yes, I may have had some other family members who cared, but I had lost contact with them, and during that time of me losing everything, I was embarrassed because I did not want to feel like a charity case because I was always taught to hold my own no matter what and to depend on yourself only. But I had fallen. Well, I was wounded. I was hurt and confused, and I was trying to figure out how I was going to make it with five boys and a husband who all were depending on me for support and care, while at the same time, I was trying to nurse myself back to health.

But I have to say that it was during this point of my life when I began to realize that there is indeed a God in heaven because ain't no way in this world I could have made it mentally by myself. So I did have someone. That someone helped me stay sane and strong through it all. "I can do all things through Christ who strengthens me" (Philippians 4:13 King James Version, Bible Gateway). And indeed, I do, and I am still doing it! All praises to my heavenly Father!

Well, my five boys and my husband at that time ended up being homeless. For one reason, we both were not able to work due to the injuries that we both had sustained from the accident. My husband was partially disabled and me, I struggled with memory, concentration, and I was in pain all the time, which meant we were unable to work, and the only income we were getting was his disability check and some child support, which wasn't much at all. But something was better than nothing.

I can remember when one of my sons had gotten sick during that time. He was diagnosed with having diabetes type I. While were going through that, that hit me hard. And when we had spoken to the social worker after he was admitted to the hospital, she sat down and talked with us about his care and making sure we had everything we needed concerning my son.

She asked me this question, "How are y'all making it off the income that's coming in?"

All I could do was to say, "Yeah, I know what you mean."

She was baffled. But the good Lord saw us through. Yes, he did! (That's how we were making it.) So financially, we were one step away from being homeless anyway. And then about four years after the accident, a tornado hit my home. The home that I had worked so hard for. The home that I bought all by myself after coming from a domestic violence shelter was no longer habitable, and I had no money or no help from anyone to help me save my home. I did have insurance on my home, but I ended up losing it from fraud.

You know, it was during that time when adjusters came out and tried to help you with getting you're taken care of. But by me not knowing what to do and trying to keep my mind stable, I chose this guy from my home from down south Louisiana, and he took off with my insurance money! How about them apples? During that time, my thoughts were racing. They were pounding. What do I do? How do I do it and when? Oh, God, you have to help me. Five boys and a husband. I can't do it alone! Yes, I feel so all alone sometimes, but one thing is that I knew that I was not alone because I know, Father, you are with me.

Sometimes I have often wondered where I would be if I had not come from a place that was dysfunctional. I often wonder if my life would have been better if I would have made better choices based on a healthy environment or maybe not. Who knows? Only God knows. I often felt like where am I? Or where did I go wrong? I want so much for my boys to be a success in this life. Do I want too much? Should I just let go and let them go for what they know? Or maybe I should ley my husband go and be free so that he can have peace. (This was on a day that I was feeling overwhelmed: June 27, 2011. So you see, I have been in this thing for a long time, and I have been writing ever since 2005, give or take a year or two. June 13, 2014, the thoughts that were in my mind during the life's changes, I have been married now for about six years, and ask me now. Do I still feel the same way inside about this man? No, I do not. I did not see this coming. I did not look down the road to see that I would be with someone who would treat me like I don't exist.)

So needless to say, me and my boys ended up homeless again. Well, I couldn't say that I had a husband then because shortly after the car accident, about three years to be exact, he left me on my birthday! Wow! Can you believe that? I was walking on a walker with his child in my stomach, my body racking with pain, while all at the same time, trying to nurse him back to health, feeding, shaving, and bathing him. He left. He got tired of living that way. Well, so was I, but what was a girl to do? I was not able to go out and get it any more. I was barely able to walk or understand due to me sustaining a head injury from that car accident. But that's how life happens sometimes.

You know, somebody told me that he was not used to that. *Hello*. Like I was used to that. The vows said for better or for worse and in sickness and in health. Well, I did my part. I just felt like he did not do his part. You would think that something like this would bring couples together, but that wasn't the case with me. (LOL.) I think that it starts with a motive in the beginning. Meaning in the beginning, it was never love in the first place, and it took me to go through hell and back to see it. You will know if someone truly loves you and care for you when life happens!

About a year later, he had come back to me. Guess why? He saw that I was living rent free and that the insurance I had on my home helped me be able to live in an apartment for about a year. And he was living somewhere, paying rent with his disability, and he started complaining to me about how hard he was having it, and it was just him. Here I am with five boys and no income, trying to get myself together, looking for work, and trying to get back to working as nurse, hanging on, not complaining at all. I admit I was depressed and down and out but not complaining.

So I let him come back. He said, "Let's work try to work it out and start over." So I did. After the year was up, I was worried. I still had no income, my husband was back with me, and I was in survival mode. I was an injured, unemployed mother who was trying to make it with my five boys. So I said, "Why not?"

We ended up living in a hotel for about two months. We had no help from no one, and we didn't know what else to do. It was that point to where I just wanted to give up on life. I could not believe that this was happening to me. I mean, I went to church every dang Sunday, I paid my tithes faithfully with the little income that I was getting, I was in the ministry at my church, and I was down and out.

It was during that time my eyes were open to church people, tithing, and life. Yes, there were many people who knew of my situation at the church, and yet, no one cared to even call me to see how my family and I were doing. There were about one or two members who checked on me, but I was so embarrassed to the point to where I got out of touch with them because I didn't want to feel like a charity case because I was one who didn't ask people for anything. If I could not to get work, then I would just rather go without before I ask someone for something.

So now, I look at the church different now, and I no longer pay my tithes. That's another story. I was treated as if I was a prostitute, and the people who were getting my money were the pimps. I can go on and on with this, but I won't because I know this will spark a fuss, in which that is not what I am trying to do. I am just telling my story just like it happened. Whether they, at the church, cared or not, this is what happened to me.

Anyways, after about two months or so, living in a hotel, my husband ended up reaching out to a program that helped veterans and their families. And we stayed there for about three years. When were interviewed for the program, we were really at our lowest point. So we didn't know what to expect, and there was this sweet, cute little redhead social worker who was nice to us and who chose to give us a chance. That was a relief. Now I can focus, get my thoughts together and regroup because I was back in college trying to obtain another degree, in which I finally did (psychology), and I could finally breathe because my boys were going to have a place of their own again. So when we had completed the paperwork for out apartment, I was excited!

The social worker then told us that they were working on the apartment to get it done for us and that she would call us when the apartment was ready. She also told us that she would take us by to see the apartment. When she called us to meet her to see the apartment, I was in total shock! I was in disbelief! The apartment was in a high-crime area, and the apartment was filled with roaches! I was so downtrodden until I could not believe that this was where they actually housed some veterans and their families.

Okay, wait. I get what you are thinking. You are probably thinking, *Well, you need to just be grateful and thankful that you have a place to stay until you can get back on your feet.* Yes, I was indeed very grateful! When we received the keys to the apartment, I was a bit relieved. It was just that me and my boys were not used to living in an environment to where you have to worry about if you were going to get shot or robbed. By all means, I am not looking down on no one, and I never have. It was just that I had worked hard to come to Texas for a better life for my boys and to try to place them in an environment to where they could thrive and not worry about going outside and getting shot. But we were homeless, and we dealt with it.

I kept my boys close to me, and I prayed harder every night. And God did indeed keep us. As a matter of fact, I think that I was the neighborhood's mom. Because some of those poor babies would come and play with my boys outside, and they would sometimes be hungry or just needing some tender loving care. So that love I was shown growing up, I showed to those little children who would come and knock on my door hungry and just wanting to come and hang out in Mrs. Tiffiny's apartment, so it was a lesson or two in it for me.

I learned something about being in the hood with my black folks in whom I love dearly because I am black. I learned that there were those who were really trying to make it. They have just got in a situation, and they were living there to try to get their lives together. Then there were those who were content with how they were living, and they were fine with life just the way it was.

So while I was attending college majoring in psychology, I was studying psychology, living among the underserved population. I was the researcher as well as the research! As bitter as this tasted to me, I tried to make the best of it. It was okay, but the problem had come in when we ended up getting another social worker.

She started out, or she seemed as though she cared. She seemed very nice and compassionate, but the longer we had her as a social worker, she was the wicked witch from the East. Even if she was new to being a social worker, she did not have to be mean and ugly. What I mean by this is that she made a mockery at times of me. When I would go to her to share things, she would come to the apartment and conduct herself very unethically.

I can remember one time she had come by for a visit, and right before she was done, she held out her hand and said, "I'm getting married." So I went on as if I didn't hear her, and she came back and followed me to my room and said, "Didn't you hear me? I said I'm getting married." It was very unethical. She did this to me because she knew that my husband and I were having some issues, and she was being sarcastic and making fun of our situation, in which she was supposed to be a professional about what she was doing.

She also would use her position in an abusive manner. I was the wife in the program, and I did not have to go to those monthly meetings. But for some reason, she felt the need to speak with me. I did not like her persona, and she did not care about people. So she had come into our apartment one day while we were out, and she put a mandatory letter on our counter top, stating she needed to see me. Well, me being venerable, I went. I had those boys, and I did not want to get thrown out in the streets all because of somebody was on a power trip. So needless to say, I went, and I was very quiet because I was in a low state, and I just wanted to hurry up and leave. As the meeting went on, I found out that my husband was talking about me to her, and she wanted to be exquisite to see what was going on in our lives just so that she could feel good about herself, or just so she could make matters worse.

So that went on for about two years in the program until she accomplished what she was set out to do, which was to destroy our marriage. And surely as the sky is blue, my husband filed for a divorce while we're living in a homeless program. I got served papers in a homeless program. How embarrassing that was. I felt like the lowest scum of the earth. I couldn't believe that he would stoop this low after all that I did for him. Now, I may be wrong, but I truly believe that he had a thing for this social worker! *Ugh!* Can you believe that? After a while of being in the program, he came to me and said, "We need to try to get out of here because she is a witch." I wonder what happened. *Hmm!* Oh well. God Bless me. I made it through that hurdle.

You know, you would think that people who are in these positions would have some damn decency about them to not destroy families and all that we had been through, in which she knew. I didn't understand for the life of me how a social worker could do people like this. She was supposed to be a help to those in need and help to guide others to the place they needed to be in life, not to cause people to want to give up and die in life.

So this, indeed, was an experience for me. I learned many lessons from being in this situation. The one thing that I learned the most was to not ever treat people like this if I am ever a social worker or a case manager. I learned how not to be and to always look at myself and make sure that I am not in denial about my shortcoming when it comes to helping others. In this situation, this social worker was very unethical, and I felt like she should not have been in a program such as this. Oh well!

Chapter 9

Up and Working Again: My Testimony

Well, well, well. Can you believe it? I am up working again. I now have a second degree, working on my third degree. Not sure how that's going to turn out because guess what? It is a master's in social work! LOL! Yes, after all that I had been through, I found my true calling. I'm going to try to be a licensed social worker. LOL. Okay, so yes, I am now back working, and I am now in a house. I am still on a housing program because I have been working now for about two years. But at least we are in a nice area, and my boys are still going to the same school that they were going to when where living in the shelter. And I must say that I am in a better state mentally and physically. Now financially, I am still trying to build, but at least I'm not where I used to be. And, yes, my eighty-one-year-old grandmother is still hanging in here with me, encouraging me to keep on keeping on. LOL!

I must say that back there where I had come from was indeed a roller-coaster ride. I didn't know if I was going to last this long. I honestly thought that my life was over and done with, but I held on to my faith, the inner strength within along with the fight to try to hang on for my five boys. I would have to say that my boys helped me keep on going, and they told me I helped them keep on going too. I made them get up every day, day in and day out, telling them, "You got to school and finish." I told them to "not give up, and as long as I got breath in my body and there is a God in heaven, y'all are going to make it." It was hard as hell. Literally!

But we made it through, and we are still making it! It wasn't until December 4, 2014, when I made forty that I had come to the point wondering where do I go now. What do I do? I would constantly and daily talk to my father in heaven, asking for guidance because the first part of my life was literally a mess! Now that was a ride! Ha ha ha. (I am laughing now because I can now do that freely!)

I felt like my life was just passing on by. I often have had the thoughts of what's the point when you try to do what you can when it seems as if you are never going to get out of your situation you are in whether it was by trials and tribulations, or whether it was by your own hands unconsciously (not knowing) or consciously (knowing). But for some odd reason, I kept on going. I kept on pushing in hopes of a divine turn around because this was the only thing that could help me now. I now look back over my life in every way possible and wonder how I made it through. I thought that trying to be with someone and love them would be the answer to the turmoil inside, being that I had come from abuse growing up, but, boy, was I wrong. It turned out that he was not the answer either.

I know that this book may be a little different from most. I chose to use myself in my story instead of using fake characters, and I chose to keep it real and share with you, the reader, that even though the struggle is real, you can make it if you try. Just change your mind a little bit, maybe change some of the company you keep, keep your eyes on the prize, and you will see that you are doing the thing! LOL!

Well if you are wondering, was I writing this book out of trying to get back at those who have hurt me? Was I trying to gain something from putting my story out there like this? Well, the answer is no. I am writing this book for myself. I am writing this so that I can be completely free but most of all, to touch that lost soul who maybe is really trying to figure it out. I am writing this also for you because if I can make it through life's heartaches, setbacks, and mishaps, so can you.

Just let it all go and focus and look up, and you will see that the sun will indeed shine again! Always stay hopeful! Always stay positive no matter what situation you may find yourself in and always say a prayer. I found that it really works! LOL! And before long, as you look around, you will see that you have made it on up the road a little bit further and a little bit better. Just know if you keep your head up, fight, push, and stand, you will smile again! Forget about the negativity and let it all go! Live! Love! Laugh and hold on to your faith! Do not give up! I know! LOL!

Prayer

————————◦◦◦————————

Here is a little prayer for you, for whoever reads my book. May you, Father, help them, heal them, deliver them, and set them free! Bless them! In Jesus's name. Amen!

My mother, the one who reared me up the best way that she knew how. At a young age (16), she decided to make the choice to bring me here. She told me once that she had to answer to God if she did not bring her children up in the way of The Lord.

"Proverbs 22:6 KJV—Train up a child in the way that he should go, and when he is old he will not depart from it." Biblegateway.com

Well she meant that. Day in and day out she would preach and preach to her children to do right, and to live right. She taught us to be kind to others and never mistreat anyone no matter their creed, color, or status. She taught us to love all mankind and to never throw trash on the ground. Lol!

She taught us to be good citizens and to take care of where you live and always take care of your family first. She would always say," Charity starts at home." She showed us what a mother's role was in the home.

Hurting inside herself and trying to figure out who she was, she did the best that she humanly could to bring her children up in a Godly way. I say this because this is something that was driving her inside, and I must say that I got the picture now, and that if it were not for her teaching me the things she taught me as well as morals and values, I don't know where I would be. I would have to say that for me what she gave me was priceless. What she taught me saved my life, and as her oldest daughter I am very grateful.

There were some things I mentioned in the book about how she may have done some things to me that she did to me that was hurtful when it had come to a couple of relationships as well as some other things, but she told that she did what she did out of not wanting to let me out of the nest. Instead of this mother eagle not wanting to push me out of the nest, she tried to keep me in the nest. She told me she did not want to let me go.

Momma thank you for what you did and May God Bless you for bringing me up in the way of The Lord.

Love Tiffiny

Mrs. Tammie Lynch (Prophetess)

My Grandmother's Memoir: Her Words to Me in 2019

I love you, Momma. From Tiffiny.

Her words filled with love and encouragement were, are, and will always be dear to me. It was her love and my faith in the good Lord who helped me overcome when I was down and out in the valley low!

May 30, 2019

He will open doors no man can close. He won't let you suffer when you're his. You may go without, but he won't let you suffer. I thank the Lord I hoped somebody. My living ain't in vain. Now, I can walk on out. (She started laughing.)

When it comes to you and somebody doing right by you, it matters. Tell God about it.

She said she helped Apostle Hezekiah back in the days because he was the right person for the congregation and so I helped him. Apostle Hezekiah is a prophet I grew up with, and I remember him always coming around, telling us the truth and not lying to us. She had respect for him because he wasn't like a lot of other people who claimed to be apostles and prophets. He was and still is the real deal until this day because of the love he has in his heart for Yah's kingdom and to see people free from misuse and abuse. He wants to see people happy. (He is the apostle who I mentioned in my book in the beginning, and the same one whose picture will also be in the book also.)

She said, "Family should be loving when something comes up." (She means when one goes through something just as she did with me when I lost everything but my mind. She held on to me and encouraged me, and she called me every day from 2010 when I was in that real bad accident to help me hang on to the this life I was clinging to when no one else would. And to that, I am so very grateful to my God in heaven for blessing me with such a grandmother as Ms. Jimmie Lee Edwards-Jones.)

It's good to know somebody who knows somebody who can put you on the right track with God. (She was talking about Apostle Hezekiah.)

He's a good God! He looks out for his folks too. He won't let you go down the drain and you his. She talked about David in the Bible.

It's good to know you got the Lord to depend on, but you have to live right before him.

We don't have to be low down. (She said this about how we should not treat people.)

We may not have some things that people have, but we have some things they don't have. Some people are not happy and got everything, but that's the way it is. (She started laughing.) Those are the things we have to think about.

Sometimes you lay down you feel so all alone. I know how you think I feel.

You know how to get the things you want from the Lord. He can put you in the right order.

Sometimes you get tired in the army of the Lord.

Some people in these churches be talking about a lot of stuff, but it's one Lord and one Jesus over us all!

We rather have joy than cussing and hollering. (LOL.)

She said, "You have so many things to be thankful for that others have been through." (She was talking about what she went through with her kids and their daddy, and how she would go to his house and ask him for money.) But she held on and worked two to three jobs by herself to take care of six children. (A woman-and-a-half, my grandmother.)

We thank him for taking care of us, seeing that out kids are taken care of. He's got the power!

I can't have a heart like that. (A bad heart.) She said, "I just can't do it!" She said, "The old lady is eighty-two. That's a good life. I want him to keep me in the right path, and if the ship is sinking, he will keep me on the right path."

You can't pour water on a drowning mane. (Meaning if somebody is already down drowning and sinking, why pour more water on him/her? She dedicated her life to help people, and she taught us to do that whether all of us in the family do it or not we were taught to help people.)

May 31, 2019

When God helps you, nobody can stop it! We want to see other folks happy. I like to see people happy, and when you see people and if you are able to help them do it and move on whether they are child of God or the devil, you help them, and God will take care of the rest

She said she wants to be clean when she goes to sleep.

You got to try to draw people to God so they can know what they're doing. Some act like they stuck up and know everything, but that's a lie. Don't none of us know everything. I want to see people happy. We all should want to see people happy and not just our family.

If you help people and talk to them, they may turn out to be a child of God. (They may change is what she was saying.)

I was going through a tough time. (It seemed as though I was always going through a tough time), and she told me this, "Pray to God and trust him and do good, and he will take care of you."

Talk to him every day. He's with you.

Did you pray today? How did you feel? (She asked me in a very loving and caring tone.)

God is good! He's been good to me! I prayed my last days be my good days.

June 01, 2019

How are you doing today? Are you still hanging on? I said yeah. And I asked her how she's doing, and she said, "I'm hanging."

June 02, 2019

He will stay with you as long as you stay on the path to do right.

She said, "You soothe me when I talk to you." She said, "That's all you need is somebody to soothe you and your Bible. It soothes you!

"See, Tiffiny, I'm in age you are coming to God, and you want to do the things pleasing to him. You may want to do things foolish, but he will let you know when you are wrong. Don't think you are lost.

"Just think of the things we talk about. And I love you, Tiffiny. Have a good night!"

I told her, "I love you too. And you have a good night too!"

Apostle Thomas Hezekiah and First Lady Hezekiah from
Turning Point Ministries, Lake Charles, Louisiana

What can I say about this man of Yah right here? This real deal
true prophet of the most high who has a heart for the kingdom of
Yahweh and for people. I have never met one such as this pastor from
Lake Charles, Louisiana. I remember when I was a little girl, and he
would come by my grandmother's house always smiling and telling
people what thus saith the Lord, and he never bowed down from a
fight. He was always telling you the truth no matter if it hurt you or
him, but he would do it in love because he loves people, and he, too,

wants to see people happy and free from bondage and to live the life we are purposed to live according to God's Word.

Some years had passed, and I had gotten out of touch with him because I knew that he was going to know that I was not living right. And he was going to tell me. LOL. But it was when my grandmother got down sick, and I reached out to him to let him know what was going on with her because he was so dear to her. And she helped him along the way some years back. I told him the things I went through, and when he spoke into my life, he laid his hands on me to pray for me things in my life started shifting and changing for the better.

And no, I did not give him any money! *Whoa*! Can you believe that? The reason why I say this is because whenever I would see him, he would always give me his blessings and speak life into my situation and pray for me, and I never gave him anything, in which I had belonged to a couple of really big churches in my life and time and paid my tithes and gave offerings, served on the ministry, and it seemed as if or as though my life was at a standstill. I kept waiting and hoping for something to happen, but nothing what they were talking about happened. A house, a car, a good husband, a business, a circle of a good support group to help encourage me along the way—none of that. As a matter of fact, things got worse! That's when the accident happened and all that other good stuff I was talking about earlier.

I was just waiting and waiting and giving and giving, but the only thing I got was what you want when a crisis happened to me and my family when I went to the church for a little help. *No.* I didn't go every day or every week. It was once or twice when I lost my home to a tornado and when I lost my job due to me not being able to work, but nothing was never said when I was giving my money for years. Oh well, another story another time. But anyway, you get my drift. Not to knock nobody's living. LOL. Just to tell you what I experienced and what happened to me, that's all. And no, I'm not even mad. I'm so over that.

It wasn't until I had gotten back in contact with the apostle that things had begun to break off my life. And I told him one day that "I thank Yah in heaven for you because you are real, and you tell us the truth because you have love in your heart." No matter what he goes through, he still stands and encourages people, and to that, I am very grateful. I told him that no, it's not about money, but from now on, I will bless this man of God because he really goes through because he tells people the truth in love, and sometimes people go to him when they need an honest or a life changing reply, but they never showed him any appreciation and love. I mean, yes, we all go through. And, no, I'm not saying pay for the word, but I think that it's good to really bless those who are genuine in the Lord versus those who just keep on feeding you false hope, and they are the ones prospering and not you. And my friends, that is so not right.

So from this point on, I will bless his hands because he took the time out to show genuine love to me and my family. And this is something you don't find every day. So if you happen to be out and about in the area of Lake Charles, Louisiana, stop by Turning Point Ministry for a visit, and when you done, bless the chef! LOL. It will be well worth it! I know! LOL! I know! Don't worry about the size because you will miss out if you look at that.

Bless you apostle and your lovely wife with her beautiful voice and your children forevermore. I'm so glad *Yah* sent you in my path. Keep on keeping it real! Tiffiny!

My life as I knew it once was no more. Through life's hardships, setbacks, mishaps, disappointments, misuse, and abuse I made it. It was through my inner strength and my faith that I was able to overcome those obstacles. Through mind-boggling situations that could have destroyed my state of mind, broken my spirit, and left me hopeless, I held on tirelessly and relentlessly to the life that I envisioned and prayed for. I refused to give up on life, myself, my kids, my goals, and most of all, my will to help others to overcome some of life's treacherous terrains. I remained optimistic for my life so that I could be an inspiration to others who are going through unbearable situations that they may feel are impossible to overcome as well as to show my children that no matter what happens, you got to keep on moving, and you got to keep on pushing.

I kept on working, I kept on fighting, I kept on pushing, I kept on praying, I kept holding on, and I am still holding on. Through my life's autobiography, my goal is to reach those who are at that point of giving up on themselves as well as life overall by letting them know that if you keep pushing, keep the faith, keep praying, and try to be positive, in which I know sometimes is so very hard, you, too, will and shall overcome the unthinkable.

To my friend, Prophetess Sister Linda, one of my grandmother's dearest friends. I thank God for such a soul as you. Ever since I was a little girl, you would always have a beautiful smile on your face. I never saw you upset, angry, or mad. You were always encouraging, loving, and always telling me the truth, and you always prayed for me and with me. You also were always with your three beautiful children, raising them the best way you knew how. No matter how hard it was, you stayed by their side. What a beautiful mother you were and still are. May God truly and richly bless your life.

—Tiffiny

Apostle Greg Washington is a man of God who helped labored with me when I was heartbroken. He helped me financially when he could spiritually, as well as mentally, during that time of my life when I had moved back from Las Vegas. He, too, would also encourage me and pray with me, telling me that one day things were going to get better for me and to keep on pushing. You always believed in me, and you were always smiling when I saw you, even when you were going though yourself. Thank you, Brother Greg, for your genuine love, and telling me the truth even if the truth didn't feel well to me when I was not at myself at one point in my life. May God truly bless you and your beautiful wife and children for what you have done for me.

—Tiffiny

About the Author

Tiffiny N. Jones is from Winnsboro, Louisiana. She is a mother of five beautiful boys. She is a nurse. She has been a nurse for sixteen years. She has a bachelor's degree in psychology and is now pursuing a master's degree in social work. She has done some advocacy work: National Council of Family and Juvenile Court Judges for domestic violence families because she is a survivor of domestic violence. She also did some advocacy for Texas Council on Family Violence in which she did a video for the child support division on domestic violence in relation to child support. She attends Thy Kingdom Come Int. House of Prayer.

CPSIA information can be obtained
at www.ICGtesting.com
Printed in the USA
BVHW031338260423
663002BV00007B/654